Bluffton Anthology
A creek runs through it

Essays on a small Ohio town
collected by Fred Steiner

Plus an insightful chapter on Bluffton
in the 1950s by Rudi Steiner

Fred Steiner

Published by Workplay Publishing
Newton, Kansas 67114
Workplaypublishing.com

This book is a creation of the Bluffton Icon
www.blufftonicon.com

ISBN
978-1-7343946-2-7
1-7343946-2-5

Front cover and back cover design by Jill Steinmetz
Body text in Adobe Caslon Pro

PRINTED IN THE UNITED STATES OF AMERICA

Dedicated to Charles Hilty
who shaped my interest
in small-town journalism
and Bluffton oral history

Table of Contents

Introduction

What me – worry?

Three conversations with...

The first Pirate

Bluffton's past perfect

Bluffton Askew

127 Making a point

Gordon E. Alderfer, Lauren Canaday, Dave Bracy, Diana Hilty Marshall, Jamil Bazzy, Amanda Rhonemus, Scott Hey, Tim Neufeld, Jessica Edmiston, Joe Goodman, Richard Minck, Alee Gratz-Collier, Courtney Goode, Micah Sommer, Ben Kruse, James Pannabecker, Sam Diller, Jeremy Szabo, Jaye Bumbaugh

Living where we live

Introduction

Tobias Buckell on a place that once was

Fred caught me a little off guard when he asked me to write an introduction to this collection of Bluffton essays. It shows you how long I've lived in Bluffton that I thought, "But I'm a newcomer!" Yet, after a little reflection, I realize I've lived in Bluffton for almost 25 years. Maybe I'm not a newcomer anymore?

I first came to Bluffton as a student at the university (back then it was still called a 'college'). Fellow students unfamiliar with my very much non-Swiss, non-Germanic last name and lack of connections to the area tried to find a link to me.

"Where did you grow up?"

"Grenada," I'd say.

"Grenada?"

"West Indies."

Often that answer still got me blank looks, so I defaulted quickly to 'the Caribbean, I'm from the Caribbean.'

My parents were neither missionaries nor in the military. My mother's family hailed from London. My grandfather abandoned sailing up and down the Thames and bundled his family aboard a large yacht to sail over the horizon to see the world. He ended up crossing the Atlantic to bounce around the Caribbean. And my father's family are local fisherman and sailors who skirted reefs throughout the Grenadines, a small scattering of islands between Grenada and the island of St. Vincent in the very southern tip of the Caribbean.

I came to the U.S. after a series of hurricanes destroyed the boat my family lived on, and we moved to Akron from the Virgin Islands (they're near Puerto Rico, at the top of the Caribbean curve) to stay with my stepdad's parents while we got back on our feet after losing everything. I came to Bluffton for an education. At the university students were required to take a cross-cultural trip to graduate, and I wrote a paper arguing that Bluffton was my cross-cultural experience, what I viewed as a temporary stay before I returned to the ocean.

Somehow, I never ended up going back down-island after I graduated, but settled here in this small town in northwest Ohio, to the shock of much of my sea-going family.

But the small town life isn't that strange to me. Grenada is a small island of 100,000. Carriacou and Petit Martinique, where a lot of my Caribbean side of the family live and I visited a lot when growing up, were islands of 10,000 and 1,000 people. I grew up wandering through random people's yards, was told 'I know who your parents are' when I was up to no good, and could walk around by myself all throughout childhood. Many people I talk to didn't grow up like that, but quite a few people here in Bluffton tell me about similar childhoods. Mine just had more beaches and spicier foods.

I don't think I would have had the space to have pursued my dream to be a working science fiction author outside of Bluffton. Here I could walk to a coffeeshop where I wrote books, would mail off my manuscripts at the post office, and often swung by a store to pick up groceries on the way home. Airports were a couple hours away, and my mortgage was not a burden on my gyrating freelancer finances. I've dreamt whole worlds while walking across town, out on our bike paths, and by the sides of ponds.

As a speaker and writer, I've been lucky enough to travel a bit, and finding a town where you have friends who come in and out of your house like characters on a sitcom is actually rare in the developed world. I love New York's many activities, but when I talk about the friends, walkability, and life I've built in Bluffton, people remind me I have something special.

7

I'm a science fiction writer. I'm usually looking toward what things could be. But this collection of memories and essays ground us in what was, and that is important as well. A town is not just a place but a community, a tapestry made out of the thread of its shared voices, stories and experiences. Whether rumors of Elvis Presley getting gas, the famous Dillinger bank robbery, or the memories of a certain generation about swimming in the quarry before the community pool came to be.

This second collection of Bluffton's memories will be reminders of a place that once was for many, and for those who have come to Bluffton in the manner I have (and maybe even some who did grow up here), it's an introduction to the Bluffton that we never got to know because we hadn't become a part of its story yet.

Enjoy.

Fork of the Rileys
Robert Kreider on creeks

Jeff Gundy was a speaker on the Bethel campus in North Newton, Kansas. As I listened, all the bits and pieces of Bluffton that turned up in his verse led me to take flight in memory. These are random thoughts that well up in the reading. That which follows is not poetry, but a boy's memory of a Bluffton still embraced by the arms of Big Riley and Little Riley creeks – these images shaped and reshaped by an old man's memory.

1 – When we moved to Bluffton our lot on Spring Street ran down to Little Riley Creek; three Sundays straight my younger brother Gerald slide into the creek; careful, older brother me was enviously amused.

2 – With feeling of endearment, we called it the crick.

3 – The wooded banks of Little Riley were our wilderness; meandering through the campus, it was our land where our parents did not set foot.

4 – Every year on the banks of Little Riley we cheered the college freshmen in the mighty tug-of-war against the sophomores.

5 – The Big Riley stunk with raw waste the Page Dairy emptied into the stream – until the town banned such sewage; fish and crabs again had breathing room.

6 – By a crumbling stone fence up Little Riley Creek, Karl and I trapped for muskrats, caught two, skinned them and mailed their pelts to Sears Roebuck for income of 75 cents.

7 – On an island in a pasture along Little Riley was a flat limestone boulder crisscrossed with lines we named Checkerboard Rock and a sandy island, Checkerboard Island. Naming the territory, it was our land.

8 – Out into Hancock County on Big Riley was another world we roamed, but one our parents did not know: Big woods, sulfur springs, an abandoned swinging bridge, Fox Hill, the paw paw patch, Hoover's pond (where we dared to skinny dip), Cigarette Creek, and the bear tree where a neighbor committed suicide.

9 – After dark, a place of romance for college students – a foot bridge, Krehbiel Bridge, with its handrails of limbs renewed each year on Clean Up Day by college students. Sad, Krehbiel Bridge displaced by a college donor's gift of modernity, resulting in a name change.

10 – Big Riley looping through town past the light plant quarry where in winter Mr. Hankish cut ice, Harmon Field, the town dump, Read-Rite Meter, the National Quarry, an abandoned brewery, the Buckeye and off into open farmland.

11 – A gang standing on the swinging bridge and contesting who could spit watermelon seeds the farthest.

12 – Gordon Alderfer telling how near that spot old Mr. Thut met long ago a Shawnee Indian who had walked from Oklahoma to see this land where he once camped.

13 – Sight of wild turkeys on the far side of the creek, this before farmers drenched the fields with DDT.

14 – Told of a tribe of gypsies camping along the creek for a day under a weeping willow tree, fashioning chairs and baskets from the willowy branches.

15 – Viewing with awe the mighty drama of flood time, the creek a quarter-mile wide, thick slabs of ice breaking up and ramming their way downstream – the gentle creek now an agent of violence.

16 – Meditating on the connectedness of water – flushing

the toilet, the water flowing down the Riley into the Blanchard River into the Maumee River into Lake Erie into the Niagara River into Lake Ontario and down the St. Lawrence into the Gulf of St. Lawrence and out into the Atlantic Ocean.

17 – What mystery of meaning lies in Bluffton being positioned along an old Indian trail – the streets running neither east or west, nor north or south. A town set askew.

18 – The entrepreneurial corridor from Cincinnati with its once 50 German newspapers and inventive types, from the Rhineland to Hamilton and Dayton with the Wright Brothers and National Cash Register to Lima and its locomotive works, not forgetting the Blufftons with their village inventors, to Toledo and glass and on to the Detroit of Ford, Chrysler, Dodge and General Motors – a corridor bonded before railroads by the Miami and Erie Canal.

19 – A few miles south of Bluffton, between Ada and Alger, a divide separating water flowing into the Gulf of St. Lawrence and water flowing into the Gulf of Mexico.

20 – Lumbermen trucking to Ed Amstutz' saw mill on College Avenue hardwood logs from the neighboring Black Swamp Forest – still with patches of virgin timber.

21 – *Bluffton transcended the local with nearby a Lincoln Highway going east and going west, a Pennsylvania Railroad going east and going west.

* Why did I number the reflections? Too arithmetical. Reflections are more like the crick with thoughts one after another, tumbling over the rocks. Take off your sandals, for the place where you are standing is holy ground.
– *Robert Kreider, Nov. 9, 2015*

What me – worry?

By Rudi Steiner

The 1950s were dangerous times for kids growing up in Bluffton. We grew up in homes and went to school in buildings painted with lead paint and floors covered with asbestos tiles. The air we breathed was filled with smoke from houses heated by Little Joe, Black Star, Jewel and Pocahontas lump coal. Our electric power came from the Central Light and Power plant. It, too, was coal-fired. Wash days for Bluffton housewives were always a challenge, especially on the days the Woodcock power plant, just north of the National quarry, blew out its smoke stack. Black soot was everywhere – on mom's sheets and dad's white shirts. Adding to the smoke, fly ash and soot raining down on the clothes lines in Bluffton's backyards from the coal-fired Akron, Canton and Youngstown Railroad and Nickel Plate Railroad steam locomotives that belched out more of the stuff.

The out-of-state cars, trucks and Greyhound buses passing through on the Dixie Highway further polluted our air with carbon monoxide, hydrocarbons, and other pollutants from uncontrolled leaded exhaust emissions. Each fall we raked our leaves into big piles and burned them in the street. In January the Girl Scouts collected discarded Christmas trees and burned them in a ceremony called the Burning of the Greens. We did this all without EPA permits. In June, July and August it seemed like mosquitoes were everywhere. Bluffton's Mayor Wilbur Howe waged a personal war on the pesky insects by spraying them with DDT. He sprayed every storm sewer basin and the banks of Big and Little Riley with the stuff. The prized Holstein, Jersey, Brown Swiss cattle and Duroc hogs raised on Bluffton's farms deposited tons of methane gas emissions into the air through flatulence, belching and wet manure, and the runoff from farms polluted our ditches and eventually entered Bluffton's water supply. Each week the village maintenance crew picked up our trash and garbage and deposited all of the rotten refuse together in an unregulated village dump.

As kids, our parents piled us into the seats of family sedans without child safety seats. We fought off our brothers and sisters to ride "shotgun" in the front seat of cars with no airbags or seat belts. We rode our Schwinn's without helmets, played baseball with wooden Louisville Sluggers, and climbed to the top of really tall trees without safety harnesses. We picked cherries and apples using home-made wooden ladders that had no warning labels and were not OSHA approved. In Bluffton's back alleys we explored dilapidated old barns, filthy chicken coops, abandoned outhouses and mice-infested woodsheds. We waded in Riley Creek, drank Bluffton water from a garden hose and went swimming in a quarry with fish and bacterial contaminates. We even knew kids who left their houses in the morning and never returned home until the street lights came on.

But Bluffton was really much safer than it was dangerous. We watched out for each other. Our grandparents, aunts, uncles and cousins were often our neighbors. We knew everyone in town – including their personal business. Town gossips, Sunday school teachers and nosey neighbors seemed to keep everybody in line. The doors of Bluffton's houses were seldom locked. We entered the homes of our friends and neighbors without knocking or announcing our visit and we were always welcomed. There was so little crime the Bluffton News didn't have a police blotter.

There was no D.A.R.E. officer. Bluffton's chief of police, William "Kaiser" Gaiffe, wore many hats, but seldom wore a gun. He also collected our trash, cleaned out our sewers, fixed our busted water mains and dug our graves. In the 1950s Bluffton had three traffic lights and no one-way streets. There was seldom a traffic jam, but there were always several "village locals" eager to direct traffic even when they weren't needed. The 1950s were a time of transition and innocence. Boys took "manual arts" and girls "home economics." In 1957 Bluffton High School had 26 future farmers and 34 girls who wanted to "forward homemaking training." This was a time before Grease, American Graffiti, Hairspray and long before Happy Days became a popular 1970s TV sitcom. Bluffton in the 1950s was a real place, with real people doing real things and living ordinary lives.

As teens we were classic. We were the first generation of teenagers. The clothes we wore and hair styles we wanted were very different from teens who preceded us. Words like duck tail, flat top, crew cut, pony tail, poodle cut, beehive, accurately described how we looked. Boys wore BHS lettermen jackets, white tee-shirts with rolled up sleeves, desert boots, penny loafers and peg leg pants. Girls wore pedal pushers, poodle skirts, Bermuda shorts, cashmere sweaters, saddle shoes and bobby socks. They read Seventeen magazine and swooned over Elvis, Ricky Nelson, Fabian, Bobby Rydell and Frankie Avalon. Boys fantasized about Annette Funicello, Sandra Dee, Natalie Wood, Connie Francis – but their favorite fantasy of all was Marilyn Monroe. In August 1957 when Dick Clark and American Bandstand became a national TV phenomenon, Bluffton teenagers identified with the Philadelphia dance couples and wanted to be like our favorites, Arlene Sullivan and Kenny Rossi, Justine Carrelli and Bob Clayton or Bunny Gibson and Eddie Kelly. Our styles and dress began to reflect what we saw on American Bandstand. We were always dressed up and our parents thought we spent too much time in front of the mirror "prepping." In a time before wash and wear, permanent press and easy-care fabrics we ironed our clothes the night before we wore them to school in the morning – we had to "look good" wherever we went. We used our mother's sewing machines to "peg" our pants and girls often made their own clothes when the styles they wanted weren't available at Vida-Vidella Shop or The Charles Company. Our fashions were our own; we were the first generation who mirrored our peers and not our parents. We hung around in cliques. We went on group dates. We went on double dates. And, then single dates. And, finally went steady. And sometimes we really screwed up.

If a 15-year-old wanted to work, part-time jobs were available. Teens had paper routes, were baby sitters, worked in the family business, pumped gas, stocked shelves in grocery stores, waited tables, mowed lawns, sweated on a hay-baling crew or the on the family farm and lifeguarded at the pool. When teenagers moved up the hierachical pay ladder or moved from one job to another, they often handed down their last job to a younger sibling or a friend. Bluffton kids always seemed to have a way to get money for having fun and non-essential stuff even if it meant getting an allowance or collecting pop bottles. These were "The Fabulous Fifties" when Bluffton's most favorite places had soda fountains and jukeboxes. In these places we spent our dimes on Cherry Cokes, lemon-blends, vanilla phosphates, chocolate malts and shared an occasional "suicide." We put our nickels in a real Seeburg Select-o-Matic jukebox and got six plays for a quarter, and when our coins ran out somebody would put a slug in it and we played it for free. Mad magazine was "cheap"– only 25 cents. We were the disciples of the 1950s icon, Alfred E. Neuman and religiously followed his philosophy: "What me – worry?"

We invented the "sock hop." In the '50s school boards everywhere made teens take off their shoes to protect their shiny gym floors, so we took off our shoes and danced in our socks. Slip sliding across the shiny old BHS gym floor in our bobby socks we did the stroll, the hand jive and we couldn't get enough of the bunny hop. But most of all we fell in love with the "slow dance" and the best dance of all was the "last dance." For many nostalgic boomers, the 1950s will be remembered as one big slow dance. Our parents were enjoying the prosperity of the Eisenhower post-war era and were living their American dream. Steinman Lumber Company was busy suppling the building materials for Bluffton's housing boom. The Garmatter addition was still adding homes. Main Street was expanding southward and the once-scattered vacant lots and cow pastures around town now had new houses on them. Employment in Bluffton was good. Triplett Electrical Instrument Corporation continued to be the major employer. Ex-Cell-O came to town and built a plant to make machinery for the packing industry. Work gloves were stitched at the Boss Glove Manufacturing Company, and the Bluffton Slaw Cutter made the "Finest Slaw Cutters and Graters in the U.S.A."

The farming community was vibrant and strong. During harvest seasons farm wagons full of wheat, oats and corn pulled by Farmall, John Deere, Oliver, Case, Massey Harris, Minneapolis Moline and an occasional Silver King tractor kept the Farmers Grain Company and the Master Feed Mill warehouses and elevators full. The milk collected from Bluffton's farms went to the Page Dairy Company on Harmon Road for distribution. Every morning a Meadow Gold, Page Dairy or Pleasant View milkman delivered freshly bottled milk to our doorstep. Amstutz and Jorg hatcheries supplied chicks for our farms and the eggs the chickens laid were picked up, candled, crated and delivered to supermarkets in Cleveland and Pittsburgh. During the holiday season the mailman delivered Christmas cards twice a day. Every morning a newspaper boy delivered the Findlay Republican Courier and in the afternoon the Toledo Blade, the Lima News or the Lima Citizen. Then, once a month he knocked on your door and collected his money. The Watkins man, Rawleigh man, Jewel Tea man, Prudential Insurance man and Fuller Brush man were welcomed in Bluffton's homes. The household wares they sold were the basics for every modern homemaker.

Down on the single track of AC&Y Railroad, small but profitable freight trains moved though Bluffton carrying freight from Delphos to Mogadore. On the Nickel Plate Railroad train traffic was always busy. Passenger trains stopped at the Bluffton station every morning and evening. Freight trains, most often pulled by a Lima Locomotive Works "Berkshire" steam locomotive, held up traffic on Cherry Street when stopping to deliver freight or just flying through Bluffton as a second train waited on the passing track.

A popular family pastime on summer evenings was watching the Nickel Plate's "Blue Arrow" passenger train pull into the old wooden Bluffton station on Railroad Street. Around 9:41 p.m. each evening the Number 9 Cleveland to St. Louis passenger train stopped long enough to drop off Railway Express freight and U.S. mail. The nightly ritual began with the Railway Express agent off-loading packages from the Railway Express car and mail bags from the postal car. The train crew talked to each other for a while, and when the talking was over and the last mail bag was delivered, the conductor signaled the engineer and the two big blue and white ALCO PA-1 locomotives, which looked like mom's Electrolux sweeper, slowly revved their engines and with horns blowing, moved off into the night toward Gratz Crossing. The mail drop lasted no more than 10 minutes, sometimes less. No passengers ever got off the "Blue Arrow" and no one ever got on. Or, so it seemed. As a 10-year-old in 1952 watching the noisy and powerful diesel locomotives, with their warning bells ringing, horns blowing, pull into and then leave the Bluffton station was a frightening, but thrilling experience. It was while observing the passengers in the coach cars, the porters in the Pullman car, and the waiters in the well-lit dining car that I first realized there were people who had different color skin than mine.

As the decade continued, Bluffton citizens built a new elementary school, improved the water and sewer systems and still had money left to build a community swimming pool. Bluffton College became accredited and Founders Hall was built (replacing the antiquated, but revered gymnasium known as The Barn), and Kenny Mast, Spike Berry, Willie Taylor and Elbert Dubenion became Bluffton College athletic legends. Times were good; everyone had money in their pockets including teenagers. Everything we needed could be bought in Bluffton. There were grocery stores, hardware stores, meat markets, pharmacies, jewelry stores, shoe stores, men's and women's clothing stores, restaurants, barber shops, beauty parlors, insurance agencies, variety stores, appliance stores, dry cleaners, ice cream and candy stores, farm implement dealers, a bakery, a shoe repair store, a furniture store, a photography studio, a theater and several beer joints.

If you were a "Ford, Chevy or Buick man" Bluffton had a dealer for you. On Main Street, or close to it, you could get a flattop or a perm, try on a ladies hat, have your foot X-rayed, buy a 3-cent first class stamp, purchase a Farmall tractor, eat a hamburger, open a Christmas savings account, put an ad in the Bluffton News, pick up a day-old Chicago American newspaper, pay a fine for an overdue book, catch a Greyhound "Scenicruiser" bus to Lima or Toledo, gas up your car and even graduate from high school. If your cow needed shots Niswander or Herring, veterinarians, were ready to shoot it. There were two Dr. Basingers to pull your teeth, three doctors to make you feel better when you were sick, and a hospital to go to if you broke your arm or needed your tonsils removed. If you died, there were two undertakers eager to handle your funeral arrangements and several churches ready to save your soul and get you to Heaven. To the north, on route U.S. 25, Detroit was alive and booming. General Motors, Ford, Chrysler, Kaiser, Packard and Hudson were making cars our parents needed and wanted. Automobiles were big, gaudy and beautiful; these colorful richly-upholstered, two-toned, and sometimes tri-toned, chrome-laden monsters came in color schemes never seen before. There were colors like Hialeah Green, Sun Valley Yellow, Desert Rose, Bermuda Green, Tahitian Coral, Cardinal Red, Chateau Grey and Tuxedo Black. Kaiser was so proud of the color options it offered that the car color name was written in script letters and placed on the front fenders. My dad's two-tone 1953 DeLuxe was Ranger Grey on the bottom and Stardust Ivory on the top. In 1955 Pontiac's models were available in 36 different exterior color combinations and with matching interiors.

Dinah Shore wanted us to "See the U.S.A. in Your Chevrolet," so families began to travel the new interstate highways in Bel Airs, Corvettes, Turnpike Cruisers, Roadmasters, Adventurers, Travelers, Rambler Americans, New Yorkers, Manhattans, Hollywoods, Cosmopolitans, Metropolitans, Safaris, Nomads, Vagabonds, Skyliners, Bonnevilles and Carribbeans. There were Thunderbirds, Darrins, Golden Hawks, Hornets, Wasps, Firedomes, Dragons, Hotshots, Jeepsters, Furrys, Champions, Ambassadors, Imperials, Patricians, Commodores, Chieftains, Diplomats, Presidents and even President Speedsters. Basic "Made in the U.S.A." sedans were still Super, Special, Deluxe or Custom. There were business coupes, two-door coupes, no-post true hardtops, four-door sedans, four-door hardtops, retractable hardtops, convertibles, station wagons, sedan deliveries, utility sedans and by the end of the 1950s there were coupe utility vehicles, the Ford Ranchero and Chevrolet El Camino. There were also a few lemons, including the Edsel, Renault Dauphine and the Corvair, which was unsafe at any speed. The cars parked on Main Street on Saturday night in 1958 had grown wrap-around windshields, huge tail fins and massive chrome grills. These behemoths rode on wide white wall tires, often covered with fender shirts adding to their aerodynamics and aesthetics. Some models were available with an external spare tire mounted on an extended chrome bumper known as a "Continental tire." This was supposed to make any car as cool as the original 1939 Lincoln Continental. Probably no other automobile accessory or available dealer option typified the 1950s more than the Continental kit. At a time when gas was 30 cents a gallon, no one seemed to care that the cars of the mid-century were among the greatest gas consumers of all time. These 10 mile-per-gallon guzzlers kept the five gas stations located along Main Street in business into the next decade.

Bluffton's car sub-culture needed new places to go to survive; teenagers need to see and to be seen. Southgate Lanes was built at the edge of town on Dixie Highway. If you wanted to go bowling you had to drive to get there. Benroth's Dari-Delite was the closest thing Bluffton had to a classic doo wop drive-in. There was plenty of parking, two walk-up windows and space for kids to congregate. On hot summer nights eating soft-serve ice cream at the Dari-Delite always seemed to be a race against time. Outdoor drive-in theaters, The Gloria, The Sharon and The Springbrook were popular with families and teenage couples. Not many Bluffton teenagers owned their own car. So, we begged, borrowed and sometimes even stole the family car to sneak off to Lima. There we cruised Lima's popular drive-in restaurants, including Frisch's Big Boy, Spykers, The King Burger, the Susie Q, The Big Wedge Inn, and the famous original Kewpee on Elizabeth Street, where we could to ride the turntable.

The '50s were actually quite boring until about 1955. That was the year teenagers discovered the transistor radio. Like the cars our parents loved, our transistor radios were stylish, colorful and loaded with chrome. These 5-transistor, 9-volt wonders gave us instant sound and their size allowed us to listen to music wherever we went. These colorful hand-held wonders were the ancestors of the boom box, the Walkman, MP3 player and today's latest version of the smart phone. Transistor radios changed the way we listened to music and how we got our information. In our youth culture, music and information suddenly became portable, meaning we could listen to the music we liked away from the control of our parents. We were the first generation to hear Rock and Roll. It was our new-found freedom and individuality that fueled this musical revolution. Our listening habits created the Top 40 broadcasting format and we made the disc jockey a radio personality. Rock and Roll and AM radio seemed to come together at the same time.

After the morning Little Red Barn programing was over and Jay Gould finished his "Dinner on the Farm" and "Chore Time," Bluffton teenagers took control of the home radio dial on WOWO 1190 AM. WOWO was the big 50,000-watt clear channel radio station in Ft. Wayne, Indiana. The afternoon DJ's Bob Sievers and Bob Chase were the radio personalities we listened to. The two Bob's weren't the typical loud fast-talking DJ types we heard at night or on other stations, but they were okay and they played the records approved by our parents, who were loyal WOWO's morning listeners.

By the late 1950s CKLW-AM 800 (Detroit/Windsor) began developing the Top 40's programming format that it became famous for in the 1960s. CKLW AM, a Mutual Broadcasting System affiliate, was loud and slick. Its catchy jingles, 30-second spots and witty commercials were exactly what Bluffton and Midwestern teens wanted to hear. On summer afternoons at the Bluffton swimming pool most transistors radios were tuned to CKLW's Ron Knowles or Robin Seymour. Night-time radio was a different world. The AM air waves came alive with radio skips bombarding the Midwest and Bluffton like falling stars.

Our world was opened up to places few of us had ever been. That doorway to the other world was KDKA Pittsburgh, WLS Chicago, WBZ Boston, WABC New York City, and KYW South Philadelphia home of Chubby Checkers, Frankie Avalon, Bobby Rydell and Dick Clark and American Bandstand. Listening to night-time radio required an understanding of the law of physics and meteorology. The FCC required most AM stations to reduce their power at sunset so the radio signals didn't interfere with one another. At sunset when the "generator was kicked" and if the weather conditions were just right the AM radio signals were so clear we could almost see the lights on Broadway. From the street corners of New York City, New Jersey and Philadelphia we listened to the Italian-American doo wop groups. New to us in 1956 were the integrated groups, Johnny Mastrangelo and the Crests, Norman Fox and the Rob-Roys and the Del-Vikings. Also emerging from the east coast were the girl groups, the Chantells, the Poni-tails and the Bobbettes. We couldn't wait for a new song to be played on the radio for the first time and then waited patiently for it to show up on a jukebox three weeks later at the Pine Restaurant or Luginbuhl's.

WOWO pioneered the mobile DJ and radio station-sponsored sock hops popular at local area high schools. But Bluffton High School had its own sock hop DJ who we thought was better than any big-name radio station DJ. Throughout the middle 1950s Bluffton's Don Badertscher spun his own hits at BHS sock hops. "Bod" was a true '50s guy. He had all the latest 45's hits. He bought his clothes at the Varsity Shop in Lima, his shoes at Thom McAn and drove a black onyx 1958 Chevrolet Impala convertible with a Continental tire, which was the sharpest late-1950s classic to ever cruise Main Street Bluffton. Don was there when Rock and Roll was born. He knew what Bluffton teens wanted to hear and the songs popular on the Top 40 charts. In the era of "Jim Crow," Don introduced us to the emerging integrated groups and the girl groups. He played songs recorded by the original black artists. The white song versions by white artists recorded for white teen audiences sometimes were not on his playlist. Don probably didn't know it, but his song lists and record selections on sock hop nights in the old Bluffton High School gym were breaking racial barriers for Bluffton teens. Because of Don, rural white youths in Bluffton were listening to the same music as black youths in New York City, Philadelphia, Cleveland and all across America.

Bluffton teenagers were not immune to the emerging music of Rock and Roll. On Nov. 16, 1956, Elvis Presley's hit song Love Me Tender was released. On Nov. 21, 1956, Love Me Tender, Elvis's first movie was released. On Nov. 24, 1956, Elvis Presley played two shows at the Hobart Arena in Troy, Ohio. Tickets sold for $2.50. This was the 1956 Elvis – young, cocky, talented and irreverent. This "pop culture icon" was the one the girls loved, but their parents hated – even though he sang mostly love songs and one about a hound dog. In the audience of 4,500 teenagers that November day in the Troy Arena were several local 16-year-old Bluffton girls – Mary Steiner, Jane Alspach, Sue Crawfis and Susan Hauenstein. The girls, all now grandmothers can't recall their memories of Elvis that day; however, they all agree that in spite of the cold weather, it was a crazy day. A structural obstruction prevented the teens from witnessing Elvis's famous hip gyrations and the screaming teens prevented any of the girls from hearing his crooning. But they do remember the magician, the tap dancer and the acrobats who opened for him. If they really wanted to hear him sing, they could have bought his records.

On March 30, 1957, a different carload of Bluffton HS girls, with one of their mothers as the driver, saw Elvis perform in another concert at the Ft. Wayne Coliseum. However, my sister Mary, claims that better than Elvis concerts was the Ricky Nelson concert at the Ohio State Fair in August, 1957. This was Ricky's first-ever concert, and he drew 20,000 fans. It was at this event that Ricky's singing career began. He didn't even have a band, so he used local musicians from the Columbus area. An unknown California group, The Four Preps, opened and closed the concert for him.

During the Bluffton High School class trip to New York City, the class of 1959 saw Sidney Poitier on Broadway perform in "A Raisin in the Sun." It was the first Broadway play written by a black woman and directed by a black director. Unknown original cast members who went on to have stellar acting careers were Sidney Poitier, Ruby Dee and Louis Gossett, Jr. In the early 1950s television brought national and social issues directly into the living rooms of Bluffton's homes. Bluffton families struggled with the threats of McCarthyism, the House hearings on Un-American Activities and the "Red Scare" of the Cold War; no one wanted to be labeled as subversive or accused of acting like a Communist. Even though many Bluffton citizens opposed McCarthyism, they did not speak out for fear of being accused disloyal themselves. Concerns about civil rights, racism and segregation, unions and the right-to-work, often divided families causing unresolved conflicts for those whose position was not the same as popular opinion. And, sometimes family feuds existed when grandma died and the decision had to be made as to which of Bluffton's two funeral directors would handle her funeral arrangements. Family ancestral ties or politics usually won out as the determining factor.

We are fascinated by Americana and mid-century life style, and we all have our own reasons for remembering the 1950s. Reviving and recapturing our youth is big business. Today's automobile collector market is fueled by Baby Boomers and passionate car owners who are buying, preserving and restoring the iconic cars of their youth. In Bluffton and villages all across America, Boomers can be seen cruising diners, drive-ins and Main Streets in their 1950s time machines on summertime "cruise nights." Even present-day Detroit has evoked our memories with reincarnated cars like the PT Cruiser, Chevy HHR, Thunderbird, VW Bug, Fiat 500 Mini Cooper and Jeep Wrangler Willys. Appliance companies have refashioned retro-style versions of mom's old mixer, toaster, refrigerator, stove, and if she would have used a microwave or a dishwasher in 1954, one is available in the color she would have wanted. Mom's 1950 Betty Crocker big red cook book is now in its 12th printing and continues to be one of the best-selling cookbooks of all time.

Today music is streamed and somehow magically appears on our smart phones and listening devices. There is renewed interest in collecting new and used vinyl records, the old 78, 45 and 33 1/3 rpm records we enjoyed are being rediscovered by a new generation of nostalgia and revival seekers. The artists of today are again producing colorful record sleeves with liner notes and the new versions sometimes include a poster and a t-shirt. The record players we had in the 1950s are being built with new components. The old portable Victrola we remember is once again available with three speeds and Bluetooth, and it can still be tucked easily under your bed like a suitcase. Greeting card companies found a niche for nostalgia by creating novelty greeting cards highlighting pictures, advertising, events and fun facts about the year you were born. The cards from the 1950s are the most popular probably because grandkids enjoy buying them for their grandparents. Cracker Barrel country stores entice 1950s candy buyers by selling the Beeman's Pepsin, Black Jack and Clove chewing gum we chewed, the Nehi Orange sodas we drank and the penny candy we bought at Bluffton's Crow's Variety Store and Niswander's Newsstand.

We are nostalgic for a time when life was simpler, more optimistic and for a world more understandable. Main Street Bluffton will always be – but, not always as we remember it. The storefronts, businesses and merchants have all changed and those who linger there have forgotten or never knew its history. Hidden beneath the facades of the buildings, the asphalt of parking lots and the streetscape in front, the stores are the remnants of Bluffton from the 1950s. The bullet holes Dillinger left behind in 1933 (which every grade school kid in the '50s could find) were sandblasted away years ago. The hundreds of African-Americans and southern whites who passed through Bluffton on their way to Toledo and Detroit during the "Great Northern Migration" have long been forgotten.

Forgotten, too, are the colorful characters who presided over happenings on Main Street. Their personal characteristics, odd dress, peculiar mannerisms, the stories and gossip they fabricated, added to the color and richness found there. Missing from the doorways are the noisy exhausts and dripping water from overhead transom air conditioners welcoming us to come inside and cool off. Hudson, Packard and Nash motor cars no longer pull away from the curbs. Gone is the smooth sound of a Buick Fireball straight-eight engine and the familiar oily smell of its blue exhaust. No more musty smell of an R.G. Dun cigar mixed with stale 3.2 Carling Black Label beer or the sound of a green screen door slamming shut as a regular leaves the B & B "Stag Only" establishment on North Main Street, Bluffton. Today, neatly finished signs on shinny full-glass doors of Bluffton businesses instruct us to PUSH or PULL. There are no more handwritten notes left by merchants with instructions to "jiggle the handle and push hard," "Went home for lunch – be back in 30 min," and "Closed for Good Friday Services Open at 3 O'clock."

Who can forget "Doc" Ludwig's annual notice to those on Main Street, "Gone to the bank, be back soon." Everyone on Main Street knew Doc's message meant that he went to a river bank somewhere and would be gone for the next week. Following his return, customers could view the heads of the large and small bass he caught, which proudly hung on his shoe repair shop walls, all trophies of his trips to the bank.

Sometimes Bluffton still smells as it did in the mid-1950s. The smell of freshly-popped corn coming from Shirley's hits us at the same spot it did on Main Street in 1956 when Mrs. Carmack popped corn at the Carma Theater. The aroma of freshly-roasted coffee now comes from the Twisted Whisk Cafe a half block away from where the Eight O'clock Arabica coffee beans were freshly ground at the Great Atlantic and Pacific Tea Company. The familiar faces of the Benroths at the Dari-Delite are gone, but the smell of ice cream mingled with chicken sandwiches, hot dogs, pickles, catsup and onions still lingers and escapes through the same "order pick up window," where South Main meets Bentley Road. And, sometimes, Bluffton still sounds like it did in 1958. On Sunday mornings church bells still ring exactly at the same time. An occasional dog howls when the emergency alert siren blows at noon for 60 seconds on the first Wednesday of each month in a county-wide siren test. And in the 1950s an occasional dog howled every time the fire siren blew from atop Basinger Furniture store, alerting volunteer firemen of a fire call.

Stand on the Main Street bridge over Riley Creek on a hot summer afternoon, and listen to the sounds made by kids having fun at the Bluffton swimming pool. Those screams you hear in the shimmering heat are the same screams kids made over 60 hot summers ago. On a crisp Friday night in autumn, stand on Main Street in front of the Bluffton-Richland High School and look toward Harmon Field. The Friday night lights shining above the field are much brighter now, and the band much louder, but the roar of the crowd and the excitement of the fans remain the same as what was heard on a Friday night home game in October 1959. If you listen real closely you might hear the stadium announcer say "tackle made by Steiner, number 37."

During the 1950s there was always something to celebrate. In the early 1950s when TV came of age and sometimes the only thing broadcast on WSPD TV, Toledo, was the test pattern, Blufftonites had to create their own entertainment. Shoppers always waited for bargains found at the Bluffton Business Men's Association's annual Dollar Days. The classic car shows also sponsored by the Bluffton Business Men's Association every summer were more than just cruise nights. Lincolns with side-mounts, 1936 Cord 810 Winchesters, Auburn Boattail Speedsters, Duesenberg SJ convertibles, Packards, Model T Fords and woodies lined both sides of Main Street. In May, as it continues today, numbered tagged trout were pulled from the Buckeye during the fishing derby sponsored by the Bluffton Sportsmens Club. Tag Number 1 was always named after a Bluffton club member and was the most valuable catch of all. Once and a while a circus came to town and set up tents at Schmidt's field, bordering East Elm, Vance and Jefferson streets. Every spring, a weekend "carny" with carnival games providing cheap prizes, amusements and kid thrill rides took place in the school yard of the old elementary school. For several years during the 1950s rodeos sponsored by the Bluffton Saddle Club were held on July 4th at Harmon Field. The event took its toll on the football field.

In the pre-Title IX era, the Bluffton Pirates participated in and sometimes sponsored a fall football "prevue," highlighting the only fall sport offered in small schools like Bluffton. In that pre-season packed-stadium event two team played against each other in one quarter segments. On that one evening fans could watch eight different high school teams play. Competitors, in addition to the Pirates, often included the Lafayette-Jackson Wolves, Forest Rangers, and perhaps the Mt. Blanchard Hurricanes and a team from Rockford High School. Had Gomer Bobcats or Harrod Rangers had football teams – they only played basketball – they too might have participated. And, in an "it could only happen in the 1950s" event, Miss Flame, a competition limited to girls with red hair, was celebrated during Fire Prevention Week. The winner was crowned during a football halftime celebration. Started in the early 1950s, the annual Swiss Day, held at Bluffton College, attracted not only the "Schweitzer Dutch" from the Pandora-Bluffton communities, but also those from Holmes County and Berne, Indiana. The decade began with 48 states as it existed since 1912. The decade ended with 50 states, when Alaska earned statehood on Jan. 3, 1959, and Hawaii on Aug. 21, 1959.

Alleys

Growing up in Bluffton, alleys were important to me. It's simple. I learned from my parents that alleys were places to park when no parking was available on Main Street. This was especially true if you needed only to run into Swank's Meat Market or Hauenstein's Bakery. If we were late for church on Sunday, my dad could usually squeeze into a spot in an alley somewhere. One of the great alleys of Bluffton was the one that ran from the old grade school all the way down to Riley Street. It used to be longer than it is today. The school has grown since the 1950s and has taken over some of it. Near the alley behind Charlie Dillman's house next to the school was an old butternut tree. Any kid could find a buckeye, but I knew where the butternut tree was, so I was the only one with a butternut for "show and tell." This great alley not only had the butternut tree, but it also had a collection of animals better than the Toledo Zoo. There was a pen of chickens, a stable with a black Morgan horse and a colt, a coop full of fancy pigeons, three mad dogs and numerous sick cats, including a black one with no tail and three legs.

Dillman's alley, if I can call it that, also had the barns of Ed Good, Wade Bechtel and Bert DeVier. Bert's barn was a super barn only to be exceeded in greatness by my Grandpa Hahn's barn, which was behind the house at 216 West Elm Street. There was more good stuff in these barns than in the Field Museum in Chicago. If I was brave enough to get past the mad dogs, sick cats, rotting floor boards and mice poop I could find enough good stuff in those barns to keep me occupied for a half a day. On the walls of each barn hung license plates dating back to the beginning of the automobile. There were wooden wheels and hubcaps from cars that no longer existed. Among those were hubcaps from Cords and Auburns, which today would be priceless museum pieces. I also found magazines, calendars and newspapers older than the oldest person I knew. There were rusty tools for fixing Model T's and machines that don't exist today. There were also lucky horseshoes from every horse in Bluffton.

The artifacts in these barns changed continuously. New exhibits were always added, but nothing was every thrown away. These barns were owned by master collectors and curators who understood the value of things important to little boys. Although I never saw or talked with the men who owned these barns, I knew and respected them by the things they collected and valued. The alley, which runs parallel to Main Street and Jackson Street, was another of the great Bluffton alleys of the 1950s. This was the longest of the alleys I travelled. It ran from behind the high school all the way down to Riley Street. This alley always had really good stuff thrown out by Bluffton merchants. On one occasion I collected all kinds of old bottles, corks, tin containers and pillboxes from behind Sidney Hauenstein's drug store. My best find that day was a gross of latex balloons packaged in neat little boxes, which I shared with the Jordan brothers and other kids in the neighborhood. I don't know what happened to the other kids' balloons, but mom confiscated mine. It wasn't until years later that I discovered why.

The aromas that came from that alley still fill my senses. I could always tell which store I was behind by the smells, which came out their back-alley doors. There was the smell of newspaper ink mixed with Clair Reiter's cigar smoke from the Bluffton News, the smell of new Red Goose shoes from Walter Gratz's shoe store and the smell of freshly-baked rolls from Hauenstein's Bakery. There was always that certain smell that came from the Rexall drug store, which I associated with the opening of school, probably because I bought my school supplies there. I knew when Charlie Hankish was making cinnamon candy or when Swank's were smoking homemade sausage and ring bologna. On a cold day I could always warm my hands by the steam pipe at Alspach's Dry Cleaners. That is if the cleaning fluid smell didn't get to me first. Kids played games in the alleys. We played hide-and-seek, draw a ring around the monkey's back and a game I called ditch 'em. Because my feet were tough from going barefoot, I could always ditch Jan Benroth or anyone else who was chasing me by running down the alley between Sam Stepleton's and Francis DeVier's.

The ditch 'em game became more dangerous as I got older. This was because the game was played with cars rather than feet. The object of playing ditch 'em in a car was to get another car and driver to follow you and then try to lose the other car somewhere in the alleys of Bluffton. The driver who knew Bluffton's alleys best usually had little trouble losing the other car in the chase. My first ditch 'em ride was with Roger Edwards in his maroon 1948 Ford Coupe with a Mercury dashboard. I knew it was Mercury because I was so scared, I couldn't look out the window. My eyes were glued to the Mercury nameplate located on the dash next to a clock that didn't work. Later on, Dave Bash's '53 Chevy was the best ditch 'em car in Bluffton. Dave had the driving skill of Parnelli Jones and guts of Evil Knievel. The worst car for ditch 'em was Larry Core's step-down '49 Hudson. The car was built like a tank – fast on the straightaways; but always too big for any sharp 90-degree turns. Even though the game was dangerous, I doubt if we ever reached speeds of over 15 miles per hour.

You always ran into someone to talk with in a Bluffton alley. I learned philosophy from Emmet Schultz, how to solder a metal rain gutter from Guy Corson, and how to repair a tractor tire from Gerald Crawfis. Porter King once showed me the art of painting a television tower when he worked for Loren Steinman making TV antenna towers. Dewey Forman always had the latest scoop on what happened in Bluffton during the night, which wasn't much. I have many fond memories about the alleys of Bluffton. I wonder if the old "Drink Moxie Soda" sign is still in the garage behind the Vida-Vidella Shop, or if the "Chew Mail Pouch" thermometer is still nailed to the barn behind Greding's Hardware. I never could figure out what the two doors were for behind Basinger's furniture store. I never saw anyone ever enter or exit either of them. (Note: these were doors to outdoor privies that existed until the late 1970s. You can see them today in a walk through the alley.)

Just for old time's sake, the next time I visit Bluffton, I'm going to run my Toyota Hybrid through the great alleys I still remember. I'll bet my Toyota can't handle the bumps as well as Roger Edwards' 1948 Ford, with the Mercury dash.

Elvis sighting

Saturday morning Nov. 24, 1956, was unusually cold for late November. Despite several inches of snow and 12-degree temperatures, Bluffton school kids were still enjoying a four-day Thanksgiving holiday. Bluffton and northwestern Ohio were mired in an Elvis invasion. On Thanksgiving Day, Elvis Presley performed at 2:30 and 8 p.m. at the Toledo Sports Arena and then that Saturday, he performed afternoon and evening shows at the Troy Arena. While most Bluffton teens were mesmerized by the AM radio Elvis-hype, their parents were confused by what they saw on TV and read in the newspapers. On Friday the front page of the Toledo Blade published pictures and stories of Elvis and the screaming fans at the Toledo Sports Arena. The lead story read "The Pelvis Draws Screams From 13,125 in Toledo."

Ten days earlier the Bluffton Pirates football team finished a successful football season. In 1953-54 the Pirates joined the Northwest Conference. In three seasons the football team went from a 1-7-1 season to winning the Northwest Conference championship with a 7-1-1 season. This was the first conference championship for a Bluffton High School football team in 10 years. On Wednesday night the Bluffton High School basketball team played its first game of the 1956-57 schedule, Bluffton routed Spencerville 84 to 21. Ten Pirates scored that night, Bluffton basketball fans were excited and had great expectations for the experienced team with nine seniors on the roster: Gareth Basinger, Bill Herr, Dan Gleason, Ron Geiser, Marvin Diller, Don Alspach, Dwain Lieber, Joe Urich and Ron Yoder. At Urich's Market on Main Street Joe Urich, Sr., was proudly chewing on a fresh unlit cigar; his son young Joe, Jr., was the high point man with 17 points. Second highest scorer on Wednesday night was Ron Geiser who scored 14.

Down the street at Greding's Hardware, Dorthy Greding was in her loft looking down over the store and listening for any new Saturday morning gossip that was spreading on Main Street. The farmers gathered there were prognosticating the early cold weather and who was the better basketball player Albert Diller's son, Marvin, or Joe Urich's son, Joe, Jr? Reaching no consensus, their conversation turned to Elvis. Although none of them had attended the Toledo concert the farmers were able to describe Elvis' hip gyrations as if they had personally observed him from the $2.50 front row seats. For almost everyone on Main Street it was a fairly normal Saturday morning for November in 1956.

But then about 10:30 that morning two funeral-size limousines with Tennessee plates pulled into Bucher's SOHIO station to gas up at the corner of North Main and Jefferson. The first car parked in front of the gas station along Jefferson Street. The second car, a big blue limousine with a roof rack, pulled in front of the gas station, taking up both available gas pumps. In a house across the street from the gas station a well-known man-about-town of North Main Street was peering out of his front window. He was the first person to witness the two Tennessee cars at the gas station.

According to this eyewitness a young man with black hair got out of the back seat of the blue limo and tightened the straps holding the tarp covering the luggage on the roof rack. The young man looked familiar to the eyewitness and he immediately recognized the man as Elvis Presley. The excited resident rushed off to Richard Smith's underground barbershop to tell the Saturday morning crowd what he had just witnessed. Word of the Elvis sighting spread quickly along Main Street. Other witnesses began to come forward who also saw the two Tennessee cars. One person who confirmed seeing the cars leaving town was also a witness to a UFO landing in Henry Huber's pasture at Bentley and Bixel roads in 1953.

Three junior high boys standing in front of the Pine Restaurant saw the Cadillac pass by. Their story was that "a guy in a blue Caddy with a lot of luggage on top waved to them and they waved back." Later, after visiting the barber shop the boys realized it was Elvis who waved to them and they had seen the King of Rock and Roll in Bluffton. There were also conflicting reports. One report had the cars traveling north on Main Street. Another said they were DeSoto limousines, not Cadillacs. These were probably Bluffton College's eight-passenger fleet of Chrysler Windsors going somewhere.

The Elvis-sighting-in-Bluffton story has always intrigued me, but I could never prove that it really happened. The eyewitnesses who I remember telling their Elvis sighting stories all had credibility issues, even in 1956. But there was always the question "What if they were right?" Any attempt to follow up with them is impossible because they have all either died or left town years ago. So, several years ago, I began to look into the Elvis sighting again. I found historical accounts from the Toledo Blade archives, which described the Elvis shows in Toledo. I found and talked to the Bluffton girls who attended the Troy Arena afternoon show. Their first-hand accounts of the Troy Arena show were consistent with accounts of screaming teens at the Toledo show.

Then in 2013 I found Scotty Moore, a member of the band who played with Elvis at the Toledo and Troy concert, on his recordings and at his shows in the 1950s and 1960s. Moore had an extensive archive documenting much of Elvis' early career, tours, venues, pictures, et cetera. I was particularly interested in a picture he posted of a blue 1954 Cadillac Fleetwood Series 75 limousine complete with luggage rack. This was the car the troupe used as their touring car in 1956. This would have been the car the eyewitnesses saw on Main Street that morning. I contacted Moore in 2013. I wrote him about the Bluffton Elvis story and asked if he has any information on the travel itinerary of the Elvis troupe during the Toledo and Troy tour. I asked if there was a possibility Elvis could have stopped in Bluffton as our eyewitnesses reported. I specifically asked for information about the limousines that eyewitnesses identified. Then, through Moore's spokesperson, Jim Roy, I received the following personal response on Aug. 26, 2013.

To be honest I can't answer that with 100% certainty, but in all likelihood that tour limo would have been used (not the black one they sold as Elvis'). Whether they made a stop in Bluffton or not is anyone's guess since, but with no existing receipt or photo or anything there's no way to substantiate it, but if it's on the way between those locations as you imply it may well be possible. They would have to stop somewhere. Scotty I'm sure would not remember though. Now whether Elvis would have been riding with them when if they did my 'guess' would be no. He likely traveled with his entourage in another vehicle and I can't say whether the whole troupe/show would caravan it together or not. I'm going to cc this to my friend

Brian Petersen also who wrote the book "The Atomic Powered Singer," about the year 1956 and who might have an idea about the possible routes or remember from articles when they arrived where.

As a follow up, I also received this response on Aug. 26, 2013, from Brian Petersen, author of "The Atomic Powered Singer."

I'll have to agree with Jim that it's anybody's guess if Elvis stopped in Bluffton or not. Looking at a 1954 Rand McNally Road Atlas my guess is that Elvis took Highway 42 from Cincinnati thru Springfield and then Highway 68 all the way to Toledo. That was the most direct way back in the '50s. On his way back from Cleveland to Troy the most direct way was via Highway 42 and 36 down to Piqua and then south on 25 to Troy. He would miss Bluffton on both trips. But this is just my guess. Elvis drove his pink/white 1955 Cadillac Fleetwood Series 60 Special on this tour while the band-members most likely drove in his light blue 1954 Cadillac Fleetwood Series 75 Sedan.

So, there you have it. The experts tell us the Bluffton eyewitnesses would have seen a light blue 1954 Cadillac Fleetwood Series 75 sedan, Scotty Moore has pictures of it. When asked if Elvis stopped in Bluffton, they both agree "it's anybody's guess if Elvis stopped in Bluffton." The Elvis sighting has been a part of Bluffton's oral history for over 60 years. It would be great to have some closure on this story. If the event could be confirmed it would be as important to Bluffton's documented history as John Dillinger's $2,100 heist from the Citizens National Bank in 1933. But, if it remains to be a good story "conjured up" by a village gossip on a bitterly cold November day then that's okay, too. For over 60 years Bluffton residents have accepted the story with much trepidation and amusement. Some still tell it to new generations of believers as if they too were eyewitnesses to the Elvis sighting. Nobody knows for sure. What we do know for sure is that four 16-year-old Bluffton girls did see Elvis that day.

Rodeos and farming

A conversation with Don and Bill Herr

Brothers Bill and Don Herr tell about rodeos in Bluffton in the 1940s and 1950s. They also provide some information about farming in the 1950s. The following is in their own words.

In the 1940s and 1950s, Bluffton celebrated the Fourth of July with a rodeo thanks to a group of interested individuals known as the Saddle Club. Everybody in the Saddle Club was in the rodeos. Some of the club members were Gene Benroth, Maurice Fett, Harry Burkholder, Jim Lewis, Forrest Herr, Woodrow Herr, Millard Herr, Edgar Herr, Jackie Rogers and his dad, Roy. The club had somewhere between 50 to 100 members. Club members would have picnics in the summer at Fox Hill. There was an area there where they would play polo on horseback. They'd climb up the hill on their horses at the steepest point – and that was a real climb. Forrest and Woodrow had cattle there. One year during the picnic the men attending decided to round up the cattle. The guys would get on the cattle and ride them. They'd hold a steer until the rider was on it and then they'd turn it loose. Our dad decided that he'd try that. He got on a calf and in about two jumps he landed in a thorn bush and mom picked thorns out of him for three days. That was the start and the end of his rodeo. While the rodeos were something fun to do, they had nothing to do with farming. Forrest and Woodrow Herr, who helped start the club, made the chutes and starting blocks. These were made and stored in Myron Motter's barn on South Main Street. The heavy old things were made out of oak, all bolted together. They were used once a year – on the Fourth of July. They were extremely heavy. All the members of the club worked together to make the chutes. We cut the trees and took them to the mill and had them made into boards. We took the boards and put the chutes together and made them into gates. We built the chutes as well. A big gate was on one end of the chute. During the rodeos the gates were located in the end zone on the railroad side of Harmon Field. A gated area behind the chutes was where the bulls and horses were kept before they went onto the field. A contestant would usually ride a bull only once or twice during the night.

The Bluffton rodeos began at the Putnam County Fair in Ottawa in 1941. Jim Lewis and Fuzzy Crouse, Woodrow and Don Herr went over and rode in the rodeo. Don was 11 years old at the time. The next year the rodeo moved to Bluffton at Schmidt's field on Vance Street. It was one big field next to the creek from Jefferson Street all the way down to where Leiber's Garage is today. There were no seats at Schmidt's field, which was originally a cow pasture. After one or two years at Schmidt's field, the rodeos were moved to Harmon Field. Our uncle, John Manahan, was from Oklahoma. They had rodeos out there all the time. He was the person who brought rodeos to Bluffton. Our Uncle Woodrow, and Forrest and Don were probably the best performers in the rodeo. Woody was especially good at breaking horses of bad habits. Someone once had a horse at Schmidt's field and the horse kept riding under tree branches along the fence. Woody took a hose and was riding the horse as it went toward the trees and Woody cracked it with the hose and it broke the horse of that habit. The rodeo was always on the Fourth of July. There was nothing else in town. There was no television. That was it. There were at least 110 to 120 horses in town on that day. They came from Ft. Wayne and all around. The horses were riding horses. One participant had a white horse that loved hot dogs. The first thing he would do would after bringing his horse to Bluffton was to buy his horse a hot dog. Typical Bluffton rodeo activities included a musical keg event. That involved wooden nail kegs laid out in a circle. Riders on horseback rode in circles around the kegs as music was played – just like musical chairs. When the music stopped the riders quickly got off their horses and tried to sit on the kegs. They kept taking a keg away until there was only one remaining.

Calf roping was another event as were bull riding and wild horse riding. Calf roping was interesting. Our horse, "Tony," was bought in Texas by our dad. Tony was trained as a calf roper. When chasing a calf, while riding on Tony, when the calf turned Tony turned. You didn't have to turn him. If you weren't ready and he turned, you were laying on the ground. He'd turn on a dime, right after that calf. Anybody could ride him. He was a well-mannered horse. There were also games for horse riders. One was called the stake and barrel race. You'd ride your horse from the chute around barrels placed in a row to the stake, turn around and ride back. Our dad would keep the points scored by the contestants and the winner would receive a trophy. (Don, 11 years older than Bill, earned nearly 20 ribbons and one trophy during his rodeo days. Bill, who was looking forward to entering the rodeo, was able to do so only one year, when he was about 15 years old. His first year in the rodeo was the last year the event took place.) In another game, horse riders rode up to the stadium, dropped the horse's reigns on the ground – ground tie is what they called it – and walked 30 feet over to the fence and back. While you did that your horse had to stay put. That was an interesting thing, because some of them would and some of them wouldn't. Some of the horses would just follow along behind the guy.

There was also a roping competition. They had a chute where they released a calf. The rider was right behind the calf on his horse with the rope. When that calf took off, the rider would follow and he'd have one shot. You either got him – roped the calf – or you missed him. We'd practice roping on our farm. Special rodeo Braham bulls were also brought it. These were professional bulls and were accustomed to be ridden. They did their best to throw you off. These bulls were as good as any bulls in any rodeo. They were calm until the chute opened and then they would do their thing. One was named Yo Yo. That bull was vicious. You could only ride that bull a couple seconds. Everybody who attended the rodeos really paid attention to the bull riding because that was something that you'd never see anywhere around Bluffton otherwise. The best way to describe riding a bull is "it's kind of a dumb feeling." In addition to Braham bulls there were local calves that men would ride. These calves weighed 700 or 800 pounds and weren't quite one year old. They also weren't used to having someone try to ride them, which made things really interesting. To ride a bull a strap is placed around its belly. The rider would bring the strap up and fold it over and then hold it – that's what held you on the calf. When you'd let go, the strap would open and you would fall off. The belt is what would make the calf kick. The calf was trying to get the belt off its back. The rider's challenge was to stay on for 10 seconds.

When the rodeo came to town, we got out there and that was it – nobody practiced in advance. You had to figure that you had a good chance to be lying on the ground. The risk was getting thrown. You might get off in front or back or if the steer turned the wrong way and you didn't follow him – every once in a while he'd jam his feet and go the other way. How do you prepare for something like that? You just don't. To distract the bull, once you were thrown, a clown entered the field, probably a professional. Once you fell off, the clown would distract the bull until you were safely out of the way. The clowns always knew what they were doing because you'd better know what you're doing if you are standing out in front of a bull. At every rodeo it seems like someone ended up in the hospital. They always had an ambulance there. One year a rider was bucking a horse, which took off straight and then it cut and the guy went into the fence. Before each rodeo was a parade. It was huge. The parade came from Schmidt's field to Main Street to Bentley Road and then would turn around and come back. There were lots of horses and floats. One of the reasons they stopped holding the rodeos is that the school thought it tore up the football field too much. Whatever the reason, rodeos in Bluffton were a big deal in the 1950s.

Farming

Don recalls this story about farming in the 1940s: Before 1941 we farmed with horses. So until I was 11 years old it was strictly with horses. We had four horses – two teams. We had 60 acres and farmed 40 more acres right behind it. In 1941 we bought a Silver King tractor for $600. It had one wheel in front. These were built in Plymouth, Ohio. We drove down there to get it and we drove the tractor home. Hiram Spallinger in Columbus Grove was the dealer. I experienced three runaway horses by the time I was 11. I was mowing hay with the old horse mower and clear at the back of this second farm we hit a bumblebee's nest. Those horses just went crazy. They took off. I couldn't hold them. They pulled their bridles off and I took after them. This was at the north end of the field. It was a one-half-mile long field. They ran clear to the other end until they ran out of gas and stopped. The team still had the mower hooked and they actually mowed at a gallop for about 100 yards. And then it tipped over and they dragged it clear to the other end of the field.

Bill, at 5 or 6 recalls putting hay in the mow: When you'd put hay in the mow you'd use buck rakes. You'd put the hay on a sling and pull the sling up on the rope and let it get to the top and the hay would go over to the mow where we'd let it drop. Farming in the '50s took a lot longer with smaller tractors. You'd pull a two-bottom plow. Now you pull a four- or five- or six-bottom plow. You'd cultivate weeds, where today a farmer sprays the weeds. But you'd cut out the weeds. I was so young, that at the end of the row I'd have to stop the tractor and with my weight hang down to give it thrust to lift it. Now they have hydraulics to lift it.

Don remembers: Our Silver King tractor lasted for 15 or 20 years. It went 33 miles an hour. It was about the fastest tractor on the road. We had typical grain crops, hay and corn. Soybeans actually came later. My uncle, Forrest Herr, said they'd actually raise the soybeans and cut it and feed it to cattle for hay. Those beans were black. We had a field of them. I hated those things. The dust on them would get on you – and you were sweaty anyhow and it would make you itch like crazy.

Bill remembers: We had dairy, hogs, and 200 over Leghorn chickens. When I was a senior in high school I milked 40 head of cows before I went to school in the morning. In 1964, when we finally sold the cattle we had 37 cows.

Don describes the milking process: We'd milk twice a day. We had a pipe line. We had a milking parlor. We'd walk in six cows and would milk three at once. While three were being milked the other three would wait. The milkers would set underneath the cows and when they were done we'd swing them over to the next cows. We had a 3700 gallon tank where we stored the milk. It was big enough that we had to build an extension on to the milk house to get it in there. A good cow in a day's time will give 7 to 14 gallons of milk. Before we acquired the tank, we stored the milk in 10-gallon cans in a big cooler. Then we had a separator. You'd run the milk through the separator and it would separate the cream from the milk – we didn't know what to do with the extra milk, so we fed it to the hogs. Today we drink it. That was good milk. Today they put a lot of stuff in it to keep it on the grocery shelves. Don Basinger from Pandora would come pick up the milk or the 10-gallon cans of milk. The cost of milk was the problem. In 1964, when we finally sold the cattle, we earned $4.65 a hundred (100 pounds of milk). Now its more like $14 or $15 a hundred.

Don remembers: In the 1950s it was a struggle to make a living entirely on the farm. When I was old enough, I started to work outside the farm. Back in those days you had everything right there on the farm. Hogs, chickens and milk cows. Swank's Meat Market had a freezer where you could store your meat. That was quite a thing in those days. If you didn't do that you had to cure that meat like you cure a ham, with brown sugar and salt and then stick it in the oat bin. The oat bin was so dry that it would absorb the moisture out of that ham. That's how you preserved it. In our family, Forrest, Woodrow and Millard farmed together. Bill and I farmed together with our dad. And then my Uncle Jerome farmed for a while. Don was involved in a threshing ring in the 1940s. We didn't have enough room to put all our straw up in the mow, so we went behind the barn and built a rack and filled it with straw and that would give us an extra storage.

Don recalls the tail end of thrashing: The combine ended the thrashing ring. The first combine we bought was a Massey Ferguson. It was a seven-foot-pulley type combine. It was pretty big back then. That was taking off a lot of wheat in those days. We got our first combine in say 1946. I was a sophomore in high school. Today's combines could be 35 feet. Now farmers are in cabs sealed against dust.

My original plan

A conversation with Dr. Howard Shelly

I grew up in eastern Pennsylvania in a Mennonite community. I had seven brothers and one sister and they all came to Bluffton College. My oldest brother, Maynard, came to Bluffton College and became a minister and I followed in his footsteps. I came out here in 1946. My other brothers were Kenneth, Ralph, Walter, Alton and Sterling, who was here for one year. Margery Ann, my sister, came here, too. Her son is Darryl Nester. I graduated in Bluffton in 1950. I got married in 1949 and my wife had a teaching degree. We were planning to go to Chicago and I was somehow going to start medical school. She looked for a teaching job in the area and eventually got a job in Henderson, Nebraska, after we'd been married for less than a year. During that year, I made six or seven or eight trips to Henderson, Nebraska. Those were long, long trips. I attended medical school at the University of Illinois.

The reason I went to medical school there is that Bluffton graduates had a good reputation in the persons of Otto Klassen and Arthur Thiesen – both Bluffton graduates. So they told me that they would accept me if I would be a resident at the University of Illinois. That required living there for one year and being self-supporting, and registered to vote – those were the requirements. During that time I became a union carpenter in Chicago and just got a raise of up to $3.25 an hour. That was big money back in 1952. Bluffton was the place where I was first on my own, where I had been married, and my wife was from Lima, so we decided we wanted to come back to this area. My original plan was to be a medical missionary. We lost that plan along the way when we came back to Bluffton and started the practice.

Dr. Rodabaugh and Dr. Travis, the two general practitioners in Bluffton, were both were good to us. Dr. Rodabaugh took me under his wing and I took my internship at Memorial Hospital in Lima. You don't always do these things perfect. In Illinois you had to take your internship before you got your license. I assumed that was the way it was in Ohio, but it wasn't. I could have gotten my license at the beginning of my internship, but I didn't realize that so, I found out that I had to take my license and wait three months and get it approved. So my internship ended at the end of July and I didn't get my license until August 27, 1957. We bought a house at 564 South Main right across from Garau Street and moved in there in May of 1957. I was going to do things the modern way. I was the new doctor in town. Many of the doctors had taught me to keep their records on four by five cards and I was going to be more modern and I kept my records on eight by ten cards. Another thing I was going to do differently was that no other doctors in town made appointments for patients. I was new and modern, so I was going to have people call for appointments.

You see, up until then, if you needed a doctor you just walked into the office if you were willing to wait. So as a result of that innovation, the first day I was in practice I had three salesmen and one patient. And that patient came without an appointment and I'm glad he came. I can't remember his name now, but he was a good patient and we had a long, long relationship. My office was in our home. It was a big house. There was a large living room with an opening into the dining room. We put in a wall and cut the living room off from the dining room and put another wall down on the side of that and made a waiting room. And then we had one examining room and there was a hallway and another room. There was a small downstairs bathroom, which became the office bathroom and the laboratory. In the hallway was where you did everything else.

To start with that was fine and my wife served as my office help and assistant and so forth. The office, in the house to start with, I think was good then, because whoever came to the door, you could see them right away and fortunately or unfortunately many people just came to the door whether it was midnight or noontime. After a while when you had more practice you were never really at home and you were never completely in the office. As time went on, Dr. Huss, a dentist, came to Bluffton. He had his dental office in his home. About the time I was really yearning to get another office. He was also. Earlier I had made some plans with Lester Neuenschwander uptown to make an office. I was ready to sign something with him, but changed my mind. One day I was sitting down at the hospital looking out the front door and all at once I realized there was a house across from the hospital. Little lights went on and I thought, "That would be a good idea." I talked with Dr. Huss and as it turned out we were able to buy that lot with the house on it for less that $3,000.

That was about 1962 or 1963. So, we bought the property, built an office and moved in. The other thing about being down on Garau Street near the hospital was that the Bluffton physicians took care of all the emergencies and so that meant a lot of quick trips down to the hospital on foot. One way to build your practice is to be available to care for people in time of need. Because if they had an emergency they were grateful and the next time they'd see a doctor they'd often remember that visit to the emergency room. The other thing I did was learn to do some anesthesia as an intern at Memorial. So I was available for that in Bluffton. The colleagues at the time I came to Bluffton were, of course, Dr. Rodabaugh, Dr. Travis and Dr. Soash, who lived right across the street from me. He was going to Florida for his winters and I could always tell when he left to go to Florida because my practice increased. When he came back in the spring I suddenly had more leisure time.

Dr. Soash was a particularly nice old guy. I remember I was seeing an elderly woman out in the country and she was having some problems, and of course I was a young doctor with a lot of ideas. I wanted her to come in to the hospital and get some tests. She said, "No way," when I discussed her situation. She was Dr. Soash's old patient and when he came back from Florida I discussed it with him and he said, "Come on, I'll go out with you." So, we made a house call together and we just sat down and talked to her. He explained to her that sometimes you have problems and you need to let the doctor take you into the shop and get you fixed up. She cooperated and he solved that and for me it was an opportunity to really observe him.

The other time I observed him at work, I was giving anesthetics for a tonsillectomy. He had a method of doing tonsillectomies and the youth started bleeding and I was giving the youngster a drop of ether. Dr. Soash got the tonsils and adenoids out and was all finished and left the room. And I was there with this youth who was bleeding and fortunately, in the process of waking up, the bleeding did stop and he survived. But, I thought, "Wow." The other doctor who did that to me was old Dr. Miller from Benton Ridge. He did a couple of tonsillectomies and wanted me to give the anesthetic. It was the same story, second verse. My intention was to be a general practitioner, and by the way, my first malpractice insurance was $75 a year, and I was delivering babies, doing some anesthetics and some high-risk things.

That's what Dr. Rodabaugh and Dr. Travis were. You had to

realize that general practitioners back then did a lot of different things. The majority of general practitioners delivered babies. And so the obstetrical part was something that you really planned on doing. Dr. Weldon Diller delivered babies, but he never did any major surgery. He gave anesthetics. And I worked with him and gradually as he retired I did more of that. Dr. Diller was in Rawson and Dr. Milo Rice in Pandora. Dr. Rice was retiring and that's when Ollie Luginbill moved in. Since I was coming out of med school, I was taught that if you were going to examine a patient they took their clothes off. And so, the majority of the Swiss people who came to me had to take their clothes off and they thought they were really getting a good examination.

Having people disrobe, you must treat people with respect. You eventually get a good reputation because you give good examinations. Travis and Rodabaugh – who had been seeing people for 30 years – if someone said to them, "I have a cold in my chest," they'd just listen through their clothes. We were just beginning to get some good blood pressure medicines that could really do some good and so you had something to treat gall bladders and back pain and all that kind of stuff. By the time I moved down to the new office from my home, I realized that dispensing drugs was not the best thing because if I had purchased 5,000 pills of whatever and a couple weeks after I got these pills something really better came on the market I wouldn't get the better stuff on hand until I got rid of all that. I really felt that I was in danger of giving inferior care, so I decided one day that I would phase out dispensing and let the pharmacist worry about that and so probably by the beginning of 1970 I was out of dispensing.

It's amazing what you could buy back then. You could buy narcotics. I always had morphine in my bag when I'd make house calls. When I started to make house calls at night I asked Dr. Rodabaugh what he charged for a night house call. He gave me his classic answer: Well, when the phone rings and it's one in the morning I say to myself, I'm going to charge this guy thirty bucks. By the time you get your clothes on and get to the car, eh, I'll charge him twenty. By the time you get out there and you are wide-awake and go to the house you say, we'll, I'm going to charge him fifteen. Then when you get in there and you evaluate the situation then he says, how much is it? you say, it's ten dollars. So, that's the way it was. Now the people who are making house calls are the home health nurses.

One of the most valuable things, I think, in making a house call is you learn to know how people are doing. You better understand the situation. I always thought it was a satisfying thing to do. We had an OB service in Lima and I would watch some of these doctors deliver some of those babies and they'd use forceps and so forth and it was hard for me to watch some of these guys because I really thought they were hard on the woman delivering the baby. Of course, I always felt that I'd never do stuff like that because I felt you could really injury a woman. So I was always concerned about the anesthesia part. And there was a canister that you could give to the mother that was a kind of anesthesia mask. They could hold it and they could sort of go to sleep with it. It was supposed to be safer that way, but I was never real sure that I was giving a lot of relief. We all learned how to use forceps. In all the years that I delivered babies, I had my favorite set. They are like salad spoons. If you realize what you are pulling on, a couple times, especially with first babies; I remember one that was late at night and we wanted to get the baby out of there and so I put forceps on. I tried to pull and I knew I was pulling against a brick wall. We went ahead and did a C-section. I saw the kid about six months ago. He lives out on the west coast now and he's a lawyer. I told him about his birth and he thanked me for not pulling his head off.

The other thing that was more different in those days that we don't have any more was the telephone. When the phone rang in the middle of the night – my number was 161-W – and you wanted to call the hospital, you didn't have to turn a light on in the house. You just picked up the phone and "tell Rhoda that you wanted the hospital." *(Note: Bluffton did not yet have dial telephones in the 1950s. When you picked up the phone to make a call, a telephone operator, located in Bluffton, would answer and say, "Number, please." Dr. Shelly is referring to Rhoda Matter, the night telephone operator, who recognized many callers by voice and often knew where they might want to call.)* They (the operators) might often listen in and give some advice, like where the patient lived and stuff like that. (This comment resulted in a laugh.)

There are a lot of simple fractures in this world. My mentors in the area for broken bones were Dr. McBride and Dr. Kingsberry. I called them about things and they would say, "Oh, Shelly, you could take care of that because no matter what you do, it's going to heal." And that's true and of course, you learned to reduce some simple fractures and straighten them out and put a cast of them. For me that was never a hard trick. You had to pay attention to some principles. I took care of a lot of simple fractures and tried to reduce some fractured wrists. Most of them turned out pretty good. Concerning fractured hips in the 1950s, McBride and Kingsberry and another group, Jones and Tillison, would come to Bluffton. Of course, they had the X-ray machine. They would put the patient to sleep and reduce and line it up and those doctors could eye-ball the break and put the pins and the guide wire in and make sure it was in the right place and hammer those spikes in there. That's basically still the way they do it. They have much better X-ray guidance today.

41 in my classroom
A conversation with Clarence Kooker

I'm from Quakertown, Pennsylvania. I came to Bluffton College because I was a Mennonite. My first year at Bluffton was 1946-47. I lived in the Hirschy House, which was a house on the corner of Spring and College. The house is no longer standing. It's part of the lawn today. The second year I lived in what was called the Lehman House. It was on Spring Street leading to Ropp Hall, which today is also a parking lot. My first year roommate was Claude Boyer. We were good friends and graduated from high school together. My second year roommate with Glen Kauffmann, Maurice's brother. Some of my education professors were H. W. Berky, M'Della Moon, A.C. Burcky and others. When I started in 1946 all the guys who had been veterans from World War II were out of the army and were returning to college, and so there were a lot of older guys there.

I did my student teaching in Bowling Green, but I was too poor to own a car, so I lived in Bowling Green for that year. I got my teaching job in Bluffton by interviewing with Aaron Burr Murray, the superintendent. We became very good friends. Later on, A.B. and I joined the pheasant club outside Bluffton and would often go hunting together. He interviewed me for a teaching opening in Bluffton. The starting salary before I started was eighteen hundred dollars. But, that year the State of Ohio passed a law providing for a minimum salary for teachers in Ohio. Because of that law, the school would have had to pay me twenty-four hundred dollars. Since I had an extra year of college, they paid me twenty-five hundred. That was a lot more than eighteen hundred. There were no medical benefits and I can't think of any other benefits we had. The salary I received was comparable to other schools around Bluffton. Mary Ann and I were married and we lived in Beaverburg. That was a small group of metal pre-fab houses on campus near Bentley Road and College Avenue. The pre-fabs were from World War II. They were so thin there was no insulation. Once a big pile of snow fell by the oil heater and it took three days before it melted.

When I graduated from college teachers were in great demand. There was an opening in Bluffton because a woman who taught in the elementary resigned to take a teaching job somewhere else. I started teaching in Bluffton schools in 1951-52. I taught fourth grade and in my first class there were 41 children. The room I had in the old grade school had only windows in the back. With 41 children, the room was crammed full. The rest rooms were in the basement. However, my fourth grade students were very good students. It was a lot of fun teaching in the 1950s. My kids were very well behaved and I actually missed them on weekends. A lot of the kids came from farms. They were taught to work.

When I mean my classroom was crammed, I didn't even have room for a table. It was wall-to-wall kids. There was a brick wall on one side. There were huge black boards with chalk. Although the desks had a hole for inkwells, we didn't use the inkwells. We had ballpoint pens. Student desks had shelves underneath. When the kids filled them up and pulled something out, everything fell out. There were three floors in the elementary building. My classroom was on the second floor. The top floor was condemned, so that no one was allowed up there. I think at one time that floor was the gym floor for the high school. It was a big, open empty space as I remember it. The playground was big. There was a lot of space for kids to play. The playground had a basketball court and a large area for baseball and football, but when it rained the playground became very muddy. Bob Ewing was also teaching fourth grade and since it was my first year, Bob was a good mentor. We did a lot together including giving tests and so forth. Miss Stepleton, first grade teacher and principal, was also very helpful. We had no playground supervisor, but I went out to play football, baseball and basketball with the children since recess was my favorite subject when I was in school. I can't remember, but I think we took students to the high school cafeteria for lunch.

In the early 1950s we had no physical education teacher, art teacher, remedial reading teacher, counselor or nurse. We had a music teacher for a few years. Since we had no school nurse, we had lots of band aides and Mecuricome, a familiar antiseptic used at the time. The other teachers in the elementary during my first year who I recall were Meredith Stepleton, first grade, Minerva Hilty, third grade, Bob Ewing – and I taught – fourth grade, Adella Oyer, fifth grade, and Theola Steiner, sixth grade. Walter Sommers was the custodian. He was there for the entire decade of the 1950s. He was the only other staff member at the elementary. In fact, I had his granddaughter, Sandy Gleason, as a student in the fourth grade. When I started teaching, I taught geography, history – today it's called social studies – math, spelling, reading, writing, art and music, although someone else taught music. There was no physical education. Later on in the 1950s we did get an art teacher. The teacher was Darvin Luginbuhl. In my second year of teaching I had 38 children and I taught both fourth and fifth grade in the same room. My fifth graders were the same children I had as fourth graders. The fifth graders would help fourth graders, especially with math if they were having trouble. I think this was very good because the fifth

54

graders helped them. Sometimes the fifth graders even graded fourth grade tests for me. Some of them went on to be teachers like Vera Basinger and Sandy Diller. Teaching two grades really kept me busy. You had to make lesson plans for two grades and there were a lot of papers to grade. My wife, Mary Ann, taught second grade in 1952-53.

I remember one of the things in the early 1950s was that the school had a very bulky movie projector. Miss Stepleton had trouble with the projector. She'd always come over to my class and say, "I have some trouble with the projector." I'd go over and sometimes the film broke or I'd look on the floor and half of the film was on the floor. Anyway, of course, we didn't have all the fancy stuff in the '50s that we have now. We had filmstrips. I hadn't used one before I taught and I used to call it a strip film. Finally a couple of teachers told me, "Mr. Kooker, that's not a strip film. That's a film strip." We had at least one hour for lunch and we had kids who would go home for lunch. The year I taught in the high school, when the new elementary was being built, we had the junior safety patrol. Those darn high school kids would harass the grade school kids. I'd have to go to the high school principal and say, "Make those high school kids leave my kids alone."

The new building was built during the 1954-55 school year. The old building was demolished during the summer of 1954. While the new school was under construction, we held our elementary classes in the high school, at the college, and there may have been a few other places. The playground was behind the high school's back door on Jackson. When the new building was built, we had really nice classrooms and for the first time we had a kitchen, library, all-purpose room and a stage. I remember putting on a lot of plays in the 1950s. I really enjoyed putting on plays. It was fun. It was like going to heaven when we moved into the new building. We had lockers, new desks, lots more room in the class. It was a really nice building and well planned. When I went to college we were taught to try to do things together as a unit. One of the reasons I enjoyed teaching was because of humor in the classroom.

There's one thing about the teachers in the '50s in Bluffton. It was like family. Sometimes we'd get together at someone's house. There was more family stuff. It was different. It was fun because the teachers all knew each other really well. And, there were a lot of funny stuff that happened and here are few of those that I remember. Walter Jordan was one of the clowns in the class. One day he made an airplane. We were doing English and were writing letters. All of the sudden Walter was done and he made an airplane and sailed it across the room. I said, "Walter, what are you doing?" He replied, "I'm sending my letter airmail." You know, incidentally, Walter made a career in the U.S. Air Force and I asked him later how he became interested in getting into the Air Force. He said, "Well, you got me interested." "How did I do that?" I asked. "In the fourth grade you showed me how to draw an airplane and that got my interest in airplanes," he told me. In my first year of teaching I had twins – Connie and Nancy Patterson. They were kind of jokers. In the first week of school they switched seats on me and I said, "You're in the wrong seat." They were a little bit astonished that I could tell them apart that quick. Once a student brought me a pig's tail in a little box. It was supposed to be a present. It had a ribbon on it. The pig's tail was a little ripe. It was a joke. One morning before school started Minerva Hilty asked Bob Ewing and me to look at one of her boys because she said that he was acting pretty strange. So, Bob and I looked at the student and said, "This kid's drunk." She said, "No!" She didn't believe us until we opened up his desk and found small empty bottles of whiskey. He had raided his dad's whiskey cabinet before coming to school.

The first Pirate

And other sports stories

"Because I couldn't go for three." So said Woody Hayes following a two-point conversion attempt against Michigan, when OSU was winning handily. We aren't aware if any Bluffton coach held that philosophy. We do know plenty of Pirate and Beaver fans who subscribed to it. The following essays recall an assortment of players, games and situations filed in the attic of our Pirate and Beaver sports memory. Somehow John Dillinger even shows up in the chapter, and you'll see how a few stories from now.

Bluffton's first Pirate; the rest is history
BY FRED STEINER

The Holy Grail of Bluffton High School athletics is gone and we didn't even get to say goodbye. John Hartzler – not a Bluffton household name today – died at age 100 in January, 2013. Who was John Hartzler? Why does his death matter? Here's the answer: In the dawn of Bluffton High School athletics the school played an independent schedule in all sports. Its team colors were red and white, but those teams were not called the Pirates. They had no mascot. When and why Bluffton embraced red and white is itself a mystery. We know it took place prior to the 1913-14 school year, but that's all we know. How do we know that? Because the Del Gratz family has the girls' basketball uniform that Del's grandmother Fannie (Lauby) Gratz wore. Guess the colors of that uniform: red and white. To further confirm this, Jack Berry, who played on the great 1923 BHS football team, related this football cheer from 1923: "Red and White, fight, fight!" Ron Geiser, BHS sport historian, has scoured every Bluffton News backward from the mid-1910s and never found the smoking gun news item that stated the year or reason why Bluffton took the red and white colors. We'll probably never know the origins of the colors.

However, we do know how, why and when Bluffton High School's mascot became the Pirate. Here's where John Hartzler comes in. The following account is from the last-ever reunion of the Bluffton High School class of 1929. The remaining class members met at Vernice Davis's residence on Main Street in the early 1990s. I attended that reunion to take a class photo. Here's the story that was told at that reunion: Wallace Miller, a member of the class of 1929, came up with the Pirate idea. He approached Norman Triplett, president of the school council that school year. Triplett suggested that Miller present the Pirate idea to the council. The student council liked and voted in favor of the Pirate. Why did he suggest Pirate? John Hartzler, a member of the class of 1929 who stood 6-6 was the center of the boys' basketball team during the 1928-29 season. His high school nickname was "Long John Silver." You may see what's coming. The 1928-29 team, led by Hartzler, was undefeated. This unbeaten record was largely a part of Hartzler's role. In 1929 after every basket, the ball went back to the center court for a jump ball. With a 6-6 guy in the center ring, you might imagine why Bluffton won all the tips and games. The great team of 1928-29 advanced to the Class B state high school basketball finals, only to lose by two points in the state championship to Akron St. Mary's. With a team of that caliber, led by a guy nicknamed Long John Silver and his Pirate crew, you draw your own conclusion to this story.

Later, in a conversation with Hartzler, he told me, "It seems to me that naming the mascot wasn't a big deal." That may be the understatement of the century, for Bluffton High School sports fans, but that's what John said. I met John on his last-ever visit to Bluffton, when he was 95. He was an impressive figure, full of interesting stories and yet the loss of that game to Akron St. Mary's still lingered in his mind. The meeting with John (his daughter drove him to Bluffton from Ashland, where he lived) also took place with another Bluffton athletic legend Spike Berry. Spike's dad was a member of the 1929 basketball team. He was also nicknamed "Spike." John, who never met Spike, Junior, in his life, told Spike, upon meeting him, "You're Spike Berry. I can tell. I played basketball with your dad." And so went the conversation. John did explain why Bluffton lost the game to the Akron team. You may want to hear his explanation. It's pretty interesting. He claims the Bluffton boys were goofing off too much at some frat houses at Ohio State University the day before the game. They became tired late in the state finals contest – John blamed the frat boys. I accept his answer.

That's the story about the Pirates and John Hartzler, as I know it. I can't think of a better way to come up with the name of a school mascot than the way Bluffton High School did. Nor, can I think of a more interesting athlete to name the mascot after. Some say it takes a village to make a child. For us, it took a John Hartzler to make us Pirates. Team members of that first-generation Pirate team included Manley Thompson, Gerald "Spike" Berry, Robert Schaublin, Norman Triplett, John Hartzler, Howard Triplehorn, Garfield Griffith, Ross Irwin, Odell Alspach and Wade Basinger. Dwain Murray was the coach.

A later correspondence with Robert Kreider adds to the Hartzler mystic. Kreider said that in his boyhood, John E. Hartzler, Jr., was a celebrity. At 6-6 he was the tallest youth in town. John attended Bluffton College for two years where he, a gifted musician, organized a dance band, the High Hatters, which led to public criticism of that questionable activity. He transferred to Wooster College and married Christine Blosser – the most beautiful girl on the Bluffton campus, and went on to a career as educator in the Ashland school system. John's younger sister, Helen, would have been a distinguished basketball player had there been secondary and college women's sports. Helen was a member of the First Aid Club and Kreider said he was also a member. The club met in a chicken coop behind a residence on Main Street. The Hartzlers lived in the large brick house on Lawn Avenue next door to the Boyd Smuckers (Bert, Don, Carl, Orden), two doors from Menno Bixel (Ford dealer) and across the street from the residence on a triangular lot of Bluffton News editor Ted Biery, who lived across Grove Street from college president S. K. Mosiman. J.E. Hartzler, Sr., was president of Witmarsum Theological Seminary and had been president of Goshen College and, for a year, Bethel College. A tall, commanding lecturer, he was a world traveler who showed lantern slides along with his lectures. Bluffton held in awe the town's two world travelers: Hartzler and C. Henry Smith. Kreider said that Mamie, J.E.'s wife, was one of his mother's close friends. She taught the young women's Sunday school class at First Mennonite and her sister taught Bible classes, then a part of the public school program. J.E., who lived with flair, invited the Kreiders to their home for supper to hear the second Dempsey-Tunney fight on their radio, since the Kreiders lacked a radio. J.E. was a flamboyant, controversial figure in the Old Mennonite / General Conference Mennonite circles, with its stresses and strains in the era of WWI and years thereafter. He was one of the Goshen College diaspora whom President Mosiman invited to Bluffton: Byers, Hartzler, Smith, Smucker, Lantz, Holtkamp and Kreider.

A frozen Bluffton rabbit at the snow bowl
BY FRED STEINER

The Bluffton Triplehorn brothers, Charles, John and Don, experienced two never-will-happen-again Ohio events that few brothers anywhere can match. Charles witnessed the John Dillinger bank robbery in Bluffton. And, all three attended the 1950 Ohio State-Michigan snow bowl. Charles said that his brother, John, was being recruited to play football for the Buckeyes and watched the game from the bench. When John went to Columbus he brought Don, who was in graduate school at OSU at the time, some frozen rabbits. John sat with the rabbits throughout the game. It was so bitterly cold that the rabbits never thawed out. Here's a conversation we had with Charles about the snow bowl.

I was 16 and a Bluffton Boy Scout at the time. We went to the game to usher fans to their seats. My memory of the details is weak, but, my brother, John, knew the story very well. Besides John and Bruce Hauenstein, I don't remember who else was there. Harry Kettlewell, math teacher at Bluffton High School and maybe our scoutmaster, may have been the driver. We wore our scout uniforms, somewhat unsuitable for blizzard conditions. Tarps were put on the field before the game, but that became a problem when the snow continued to fall and became deeper and deeper on the field. Volunteers were recruited to sweep off the snow and roll up the tarps. I don't remember volunteering, but we were out there with a sizable number of folks. The tarps had to be cut into smaller pieces and some of it was frozen to the ground. Picture a line of poorly dressed, snow-covered guys shoulder-to-shoulder pushing a tarp full of snow that got several feet high. One person got carried over the top and almost rolled up. The wind was blowing, visibility was down to 10 yards or so, and as a result, it was not easy to stop the momentum once we were rolling. This person was lucky that his situation was noticed, and he was saved. This may have spawned the later rumor that one of the Boy Scouts was missing, but this turned out to be false. My personal memory was of a dense snowfall of large wet aggregates of snow that stuck to you. Specifically, when you blink the snow would freeze your eyebrows to your face and suddenly your eyelids were stuck. Easily cured by rubbing your eyes, but somewhat startling: never has this happened to me before or since. Back up in the stands I remember the wind and the cold. The game itself was hard to follow and not very interesting. It contained lots of clashes of two mobs on the line of scrimmage alternating with punting – lots of punting, because it was the only way to move the ball downfield. People fell down a lot on the slippery field and passing was absurd; Michigan did not complete any and I don't know about OSU. Michigan won on a touchdown scored as a result of a blocked punt that went out of bounds behind the goal line. I don't remember leaving the stadium, but we headed north in a continuing blizzard. The flat land north of Columbus became so uniform that you couldn't tell where the road was. Not too far out of town we pulled into the driveway of a farm house, and were quickly followed by several other cars. I read that 20,000 cars were on Ohio roads. So, a bunch of us – I don't know how many – spent the night on the floor, guests of the generous residents. Next morning came the need to feed all these people. Fortunately a semi-trailer full of baked goods was stalled just in front of the house and the driver opened up the back and provided food for all of us. The snow and wind stopped during the night and in the morning the sun came out and snowplows opened the roads, so we continued homewards without further delay. What a day.

Charles Triplehorn meets John Dillinger
BY FRED STEINER

Our chat with Charles about his John Dillinger experience took place in the doorway of what is today Do It Best Family Hardware, 109 N. Main St., and the Edward Jones office at 111 N. Main St. At the time of our conversation, in 2007, he was the last-living eyewitness to Bluffton's Citizens National Bank robbery pulled off by Dillinger and his gang. He was in Bluffton attending a Bluffton High School class of 1945 reunion. We stood between the two businesses because that's where Charles stood at noon on Aug. 17, 1933. We should point out that Bluffton News editor, Ted Biery, on the other side of the street, also witnessed the event. He wrote an excellent account of what happened. His opening paragraph sets the scene as only a journalism graduate

62

(he was a 1913 Ohio State journalism graduate) could craft. His writing has accuracy, brevity and clarity:

"Staging a bold daylight robbery, five well-dressed bandits held up the Citizens National Bank at South Main and Church streets at noon Monday and escaped in an auto with loot of $2,100. The loss is covered by insurance."

Here's what Charles remembers: I was, indeed, a witness to the John Dillinger robbery. Bear in mind that I was only 6 years old. Being almost three-fourth of a century ago, so much of what I recall is somewhat hazy and probably modified and embellished by retelling. On that fateful day, my mother sent me to stay with Fred and Zoe Zehrbach, probably to get me out of her hair for a while. Zehrbachs lived in an upstairs apartment above what was then Barnes' Grocery, in the next block from the bank. I ambled along Main Street, passed the bank — obviously Dillinger was inside as I walked by — crossed Church Street and was in front of Greding's Hardware when the shooting began. Greding's had a display of cane fishing poles in front of the store right next to the entrance to the Zehrbach apartment. Fred was awaiting my arrival so he was right there, grabbed me and pulled me into the entrance of his place. From there, we were able to watch what was going on by peeking around the cane poles. The entire episode lasted only a few minutes. I distinctly remember one of the Dillinger men standing in the intersection brandishing a machine gun as though he were directing traffic. He sprayed a few rounds at random to make certain that there were no interruptions of the activity inside the bank. All at once two men dashed out of the bank firing pistols, jumped in a car, picked up their lookout, and roared away out of town toward Findlay. All of this left a lasting impression on me, and over the years has been a great conversation piece.

There are several amusing anecdotes associated with the Dillinger robbery. One involved my grandmother's brother, M.M. (Dode) Murray, who was postmaster on duty at the post office, directly across

Main Street from the bank. Someone yelled, "Dode, they're robbing the bank." Dode grabbed a gun, darted out and positioned himself behind a brick pillar in front of the post office. He poked his head around the pillar to assess the situation, and was an easy target with his snow white hair. The mobster in the street fired a warning shot and Dode remained stolidly behind the pillar until well after the getaway. Another comedy of errors involved the Bluffton volunteer fire department. An alarm was somehow sounded and the firemen assuming it was a fire, assembled at the town hall in which the fire truck was garaged. The truck pulled out of the garage, started the siren, and turned the corner onto Main Street. Someone spotted the lookout – who may have fired a warning shot – whereupon they quickly backed the truck back to the garage. Another interesting sidelight was that Dr. Jesse Steiner had his office directly above the bank. Dr. Steiner was a big game hunter, and had a number of weapons in his office, along with a collection of stuffed animals. He could have easily picked off the robbers from his window. There you have my recollections for what they are worth. Evan Herr, a classmate, had a bullet from one of the guns used in the robbery. His father, Nelson Herr, worked in the bank and picked up the bullet after things returned to normal. *(Note: Over 40 shots were fired in both directions of Main Street by the gang, using revolvers and a sub-machine gun that sprayed bullets.)*

He outscored the entire Beaver squad

BY RON GEISER

During the 1951-52 academic/athletic season, Bluffton College had completed one of the newest gymnasiums in the area – Founders Hall. The first game actually was played Feb. 5, 1952, BC downing Ashland in overtime, although the entire building was not dedicated until June that year. One newspaper said the new Bluffton facility was one of the two best gyms in northwestern Ohio, the other being on the University of Toledo campus. To show off this new gem of a gym, Andrew C. Burcky, longtime coach/athletic director at Bluffton, came up with several promotions. He scheduled a professional wrestling event, a professional basketball team exhibition, enticed four area high schools to play a Christmas-vacation tournament that endured 24 years, and brought high school tournament games to Bluffton for nearly that long. Many other non-athletic activities, like flower shows, operettas and other musical events, graduation ceremonies, the annual Messiah presentation, et cetera, were to follow. While there were sellout crowds for many of those events, perhaps the crowning achievement by Coach Burcky, at least for one night, was scheduling Rio Grande College's basketball team for the 1953-54 season. This was the team featuring 6-9 Clarence (Bevo) Francis, the most publicized cager in the Midwest, and eventually, the nation. He often has been credited with saving college basketball after the point-shaving scandals of the early '50s. Coach Newt Oliver's team, featuring Bevo, also is credited with putting tiny Rio Grande on the map, since the tiny southeastern Ohio college had only 38 men at that time. Four buildings made up the school, now called University of Rio Grande. And his prize pupil, Bevo, was the athlete to help make Oliver make a name for himself. Founders Hall was packed with fans… estimates ranged in the 2,500-3,000 area. At that time, bleachers were set up on the stage for large-crowd contests like tournaments. This writer sat with legs hanging over the stage facing the west end foul line, small notebook in hand to register Bevo's point total. Others lined the floors along the playing floor and were jammed in the "end zones," besides jamming the bleachers, chair seats and aisles (fire marshal out of town?). Bluffton was 2-2 entering the game, later finishing 12-9 overall, 6-4 (2nd) in the Mid-Ohio League. It was Ken Mast's first winning cage team, so it was not just a "gimme" game for Rio Grande. The Redmen (now Red Storm) came out and entertained Bluffton fans even during warmups, as most of them dunked the ball and performed fancy passing drills. Still, it was the game and Bevo we all wanted to see. And he truly amazed with a turnaround jump shot from all around the key area that never seemed to miss. And when the smaller Beavers fouled him, he made the free throws, too. How could the 6-2 or 6-3 Beavers guard this awkward-looking, yet extremely skillful shooting giant? The winner of the game was never in doubt, yet the crowd was wide-eyed as Francis kept putting in shots – 50 points, 60, 70 and finally 82 – a national record at that time. He outscored BC 82-71 as the final score reached 116 for the visitors. And that was before the 3-point shot. Harold (Herk) Wolfe, Findlay College's hall of fame center, had scored 54 and 48 points against the Beavers in that era. Bluffton's highest individual effort in Founders came in 2004-05 when guard Scott Bergman tallied 50 against Anderson, aided by the 3-pointer.

Coach Mast, who coached several Beaver sports including football and basketball, said, "He (Bevo) was the best player I ever saw. He had a great jump shot. And he had a great ball club along with him. After it (the game) was over, I thought I'd just seen the greatest player then alive – college or pro." Beaver athletes on that team were Joe Collingwood, Bill Orn, Johnny Augsburger, Paul Jackson, John Moser, Vernon Weatly, Jim Bishop, Dick Cripe, Sam Wilson, Jim Benroth and Charles Greiner. Through the 2012 basketball season, Francis' 113 points vs. Hillsdale, tallied later that 1953-54 season, remained the highest total ever in NCAA play, while his 84 vs. Alliance are fourth and the 82 in Bluffton are fifth. He also scored 72 against California (Pa.) and 69 against Wilberforce, both during the 1952-53 season. In Bevo's freshman season when many of the games were against junior college, military base and biblical seminary foes, he averaged 50.1 points per game, tallying 1,954 points in 39 contests. Against legitimate competition in 1953-54, he averaged 46.5, the highest in NCAA history. To Oliver's credit, to legitimize Rio's accomplishments and, indirectly promote himself, he beefed up the 1953-54 schedule with some major colleges as well as smaller schools like Bluffton. The Redmen even appeared in the basketball Mecca – Madison

Square Garden. In his two seasons, Francis scored 55 or more points 20 times. His personal high of 116 vs. Ashland Junior College was not recognized by the NCAA. Rio was 60-7 in the two seasons, going 21-7 after that perfect 39-0 year. After the basketball season was over, Bevo was suspended from Rio Grande for missing too many classes and not completing his mid-term exams. Though drafted by the Philadelphia (now San Francisco) Warriors, Francis never appeared in an NBA contest. For two years Coach Oliver and his protégé toured with the Boston Whirlwinds, the always-losing foe of the Harlem Globetrotters. Francis, a small-town boy from Wellsville, Ohio, later worked in a steel factory for 20 years, loading trucks. He was mostly ignored by Oliver once he quit playing basketball. But for one night in Bluffton, he scored the highest total ever. Were you there? I was, and I'll never forget it.

It happened one night
BY CHARLES HILTY

Who won the 1959 Bluffton-Lafayette boys' basketball game? The scoreboard (after some hesitation) said Bluffton did 61-60, but the referees couldn't decide. One person who held a positive opinion from start to finish was Lafayette coach Bob Harter, who said Lafayette won 60-59. The whole, roaring argument could have been avoided if Bluffton's Buck Schifke hadn't been lucky. Lafayette led 60-59 when Schifke grabbed the ball after a tipoff and heaved it towards the basket before or after (pick one) the final buzzer sounded. The ball went through and the argument began. Referees, coaches, players and fans swarmed over the timer's table, demanding an official verdict. The timer said the shot was good, an opinion which was instantly unpopular with at least half the house. While the three-minute argument went on, the scoreboard still read 60-59, Lafayette, and when the final score was marked up this drew an equally loud response from the supporters of the officials. "That game has always been with me for all the rest of my life,"

Buck Schifke said this month when asked to recall that night. "The first thing I remember is Denny Smith, and you remember what a chunky kid he was, jumping out of the stand and grabbing me. He just about squoze [sic] all the breath out of me. My mom and dad were right behind him." Jim Heffner, who started for Lafayette that night and later became a high school teaching partner and good friend of Buck, says "I've called him Lucky Shot or Cheap Shot ever since we discovered that we were in that game together." Like Buck Schifke, 50 years after the game-ending drama and post-game confusion, that game has always been with me. I was the official scorer that night so I was at the center of the official melee, although safely removed from the melee on the floor. Both teams had taken the lead several times before it was tied at 52 in the middle of the fourth quarter. Bluffton then surged to a 58-52 lead before Lafayette came back to retake the lead at 60-58. Ramon Lewis, Bluffton's best player, made one free throw but missed the second, leaving Lafayette in the lead in the closing half minute. Two opposing players tied up a loose ball in Bluffton's front court with five seconds or less remaining in the game. A jump ball was called. As soon as the tipoff was controlled by Bluffton it was obvious that a last-second shot would be taken. This led to the desperate heave that hit "nothing but net" and that led to the disputed decision, the long delay and the crowds of elated or angry fans on the floor. Immediately as Buck Schifke controlled the ball after the tipoff I had begun to chant swiftly in my head... "the ball is in his hand... in his hand... in his hand..." just as I'd been taught by Bob Ewing, the long-time Bluffton faculty manager and my scorekeeping mentor since I first became an official scorebook keeper while a high school junior eight years before the exciting night.

"When you're close to the buzzer," Mr. Ewing had coached me from the start, "you start saying 'the ball is in his hand, in his hand, in his hand, in his hand' and as soon as he shoots you say to yourself "it's in the air in the air in the air." If the buzzer sounds when you're still saying 'hand' the shot is no good. If you've said 'air', the shot is good." It was simple practical advice. It worked perfectly when needed several times during the intervening eight years. That night I was saying "hand" when the buzzer sounded, just *before* I would have switched to "in the air." As Buck's mid court heave – it could hardly be called a shot – swished perfectly through the net the referee nearer to the spot made an emphatic downward sweep of his arm to indicate that the shot was good. The referee has the first call but the official scorer's call should be final in so close a dispute. First I turned to Tom Goulden, who was running the time clock that night. He nodded yes. I'd seen the referee's emphatic gesture, I'd seen Tom's nod. Even though I'd been saying "in his hand" when I heard the buzzer, I nodded. Then we saw the same referee whose emphatic gesture had led me to believe that the shot was good was staring at the scorer's table with a very quizzical look on his face.

Clearly, he was asking for an opinion. He'd only indicated that the shot had been made. He needed to know whether it had been timely. Even though I'd been saying 'hand' just as the buzzer sounded, I was confused by his first gesture and by the less experienced timekeeper's nod, even though my method had told me that the shot was taken fractions of a second late. Then I, too, nodded that the shot was good. The scoreboard posted 61-60 and the outrage began. The same referee who only two minutes before had gestured so strongly that the shot was good was angrily telling the scorer's table that "this is the biggest rip-off (not his exact words) I've ever seen." Lafayette players who had lingered on the floor later reported that they were astonished to see one of their Sunday school teachers punch one referee in the stomach. "Lady, you shouldn't have done that," was his mild rebuke. (No one knows whether this forgiving response ever became part of her next Sunday school lesson). That official scorer, miserably slow on the trigger and not strong enough in standing up for his first judgement that night, now issues the final verdict. Fifty years after the decision was made and the accompanying story was written: I should have fought for my original judgment made even before I was confused by the referee's strong gesture followed by his quizzical look. The ball was in Buck's hand. The shot was too late. Final score 60-59. Wolves Win!

Wolves Win! Sorry, Buck.

100 yards and 100 years
BY FRED STEINER

It's the oldest high school football rivalry in northwest Ohio. The series started in the infancy of the game, even before one team called themselves Pirates and the other called themselves Bulldogs. The series is so old that during the first two decades the games were played in broad daylight, since neither school had lighted football stadiums. And, the first games in Bluffton were played in a cow pasture known as Schmidt's field. Who knows where the Ada games were played.

The game recalled here was played in Ada sometime in the early 1990s. After a long series of nasty rivalries, this contest was predicted to be more of a social gathering than a night to question every whistle blown by the ref. And, then the rains came.

As I recall, on my way to Ada I picked up Benjamin Franklin. He was hiking to the game. Ben mumbled something about lightning, a kite and a key. I didn't understand him, but nodded as if I did. When we arrived in Ada, the lightning was moving south of town in a Lima direction. Poor Richard spied it and was happy. I was a bit concerned. But, an Ohio High School Athletic Association's edict sends athletic teams off the field for 30 minutes when lightning is spotted. In Friday's situation, the lightning came during the pre-game, so there was a lull before the storm. Apparently this rule doesn't mention what the fans and bands are to do. So, the band, with its assortment of metal lighting rods stayed put in the also-metal stands. Ben directed the BHS team to stand under the largest metal light post on the stadium grounds. He has such a sense of humor. The Ada team, meanwhile headed for an underground locker room in the bowels of the stadium that appeared to be as old as Bluffton Stadium. It all made perfect sense to me. With Ben preoccupied with getting his kite to fly, I bid him good luck and decided to walk around the field. I thought I'd listen in to some sideline chat. I bought a program for a dollar or was it a dollar fifty? I can't remember. Never mind that it didn't have the BHS roster included. I inquired if I'd get a refund if the game was called. No such luck, I was told. Then the rain came.

So, I headed over to the band. I was curious to see how its metal science project was progressing. There I chatted a while with Dave Sycks and Rachael Lewis, and wondered to myself if the band would play Handel's Water Music at halftime. The answer, again, was no. Midway in this conversation came the predictable freshmen band member interruptions to Mr. Sycks. Q: "What do we do if it rains at halftime?" A: "We go on." Q: "May I go to the bathroom?" Q: "What do we do if it rains at halftime?" Q: "If it rains, do we go on at halftime?" Between "what do we do?" questions, someone who I had never seen in my life walked up to Dave, telling the band director that it was nice to see him again. Then, asked if he remembered the Spencerville game several years ago when it rained like this. The fellow answered his own question: "Yeah, I'll never forget that. Our instruments really got soaked," he said as he headed toward the stands. I asked Sycks, "Who was that?" He replied, "I never saw him before."

So, off I plodded to pick up what else there was to hear. Mike Richards and two other guys I'd also never seen before were comparing the lightning delay to a time when Mike coached at Perry. His team traveled to Paulding when Steve Clark was coach. A delay there caused Perry to get home around 2 a.m. I walked off as this conversation headed into the "that year we had a veer offense..." Somewhere between Gary Bishop and Mac Davies and his parents stood Jim Herrmann and Charlie Swank. Those two, I figured, had seen more Bluffton-Ada games than any other two guys I could think of. By this time, the 30-minute clock wound down. The officials blew their collective whistles. The game began. I held out until a bit into the third period, despite an 8-7 Ada lead. Somewhere in the next two quarters I figured that BHS would pull it out. As I walked to the car, trying to think of two guys other than Herrmann and Swank who had seen more games than those two, I noticed the ONU boys from the I-don't-know-the-Greek-alphabet frat house. They'd staked off a portion of their lawn so that cars wouldn't park in it. I chuckled to think that guys in that frat house have spent more time on Fridays in the fall guarding their lawn than, well, I wondered why they didn't bother to put a fence around it. On the way home I listened to the game on the radio. There I heard that Ben McCullough (not, his brother, Sam) scored that winning TD for the Pirates. Hearing this made me wonder if I had entered some sort of a time warp, because I thought I'd seen Ben in the stands earlier that night. But, you never know what circumstances will greet you at an Ada-Bluffton football game. This year I was not disappointed.

Who said it might be a long ride home?
BY FRED STEINER

Like most Blufftonites, I'd never been to Warren, Ohio, when the leaves started turning colors. Last Friday was as good a time as any to visit there. So I suggested to Everett Collier that I'd pay for his gas and ticket to a football game – that just happened to feature Bluffton HS – if he drove. He claimed he could get there blindfolded since he grew up in the Cleveland area. To prove it, he refused to bring an Ohio map. Then, I blindfolded him, filled up his tank and off we went. The ride up was filled with the usual Bluffton gab. We slandered and libeled ourselves all the way across Route 30. We realized that we were no longer in northwestern Ohio when those little red stickers on license plates no longer carried a "2" for Allen. Instead, they carried "72" for Trumbull. That was a lesson is the Ohio alphabet. Next, the closer we ventured to Lordstown, the scarcer were foreign-brand autos. That was a lesson in Ohio economics. But, more obvious was the further east we headed those Bush/Cheney signs turned into Kerry/Edwards signs. That was a lesson in Ohio politics. Once we exited Interstate 76, we started reading the directions. The directions got us there, but they were written by one of those guys who write instructions on putting together kid's bicycles. The instructions were translated from Korean into Spanish and then into English. For example, there exists no such street sign for North Salem Warren Road. It's called Mahoning. That's even though the directions said to turn left onto it. Despite that, we arrived at Warren G. Harding High School with time to spare. We parked our car only to discover that Dave Benroth, Sharl Steiner and Joe Sehlhorst were already tailgating. Shortly thereafter a whole slew of the most predictable and unpredictable Pirate crew with nothing else to do on a Friday night started pulling into the parking lot. Let me tell you about Mollenkopf Stadium, home of Warren G. Harding High School Raiders. On the marquee in front of the high school it read: Saturday night Harding versus St. Edwards. I knew our team was good, but was relieved that it was still Friday night. The stadium seats 12,000. There was room for everyone in Bluffton, Richland Township, Beaverdam and probably most of Monroe Township. This is the house were Maurice Clarett broke in his wisdom teeth. He must have rushed for 5-or-6,000 yards there in his career. You can still see indentations in the wall behind the goal posts where his shoulder pads left dents. His cleat marks were all over the place.

Once the game started several things became obvious to the fans in red and white. The first was that northeastern Ohio officials' rulebooks are different from rulebooks in NW Ohio. In NE Ohio, rulebooks state that when the team from the NW Ohio has the ball and is driving down the field several techniques may be applied to break up the rhythm of the offense. These techniques are too subtle to mention but were very creative and entertaining for the BHS crowd. Second, air horns outside Warren G. Harding stadium are strictly prohibited, according to the Warren PD. Something about being a public nuisance. Wouldn't you know, Bluffton fans brought a remote-control air horn and mounted it on one of the buses in the parking lot. That's a Trumbull County no-no. Who'd have thought it? Despite the rule differences from NE to NW Ohio, the game was not the looooong ride home that at least one area newspaper sport's columnist predicted for the Big Red. It was anything but that. It was a night to remember. It was the night Bluffton succeeded in defeating – no demolishing – on the road, a private eastern Ohio school with its own storied athletic program.

The team hadn't led in a game in over 400 minutes

BY BRENDON MATTHEWS

Written for the Bluffton Icon on the eve of Bluffton High School's first-ever state final soccer match Nov. 8, 2020.

If a picture is worth a thousand words, then Facebook's cup runneth over today. As I scrolled through my feed I saw post after post of joyful faces celebrating an improbable run by the Bluffton High School boys' soccer team. Not only did they beat the 1st and 3rd ranked teams in the state to get to this point, but they also won four straight overtime games: three in sudden death overtime and one in a shootout. They trailed 1-0 in the 2nd half of two different games, and, according to one Facebook post (so it must be true) they haven't led in a game in over 400 minutes. Yet here they are. They'll play Sunday in the state final against the 5th ranked team in the state, Columbus Wellington. Whether they win or lose, it has been an awesome run. It would be easy to say the focus should be on "it takes a village" because it is true in this case. Many people and local businesses have supported the team in various ways. By the end of the day Sunday, the student "spirit" buses will have traveled approximately 760 miles to support their Pirates. The Bluffton police and fire departments have stayed up way past their bedtime multiple times to escort the victors back to town. Bluffton Family Recreation with Bluffton's newest celebrity, Tyler Chamberlain, have live-streamed the last three games on Facebook, and Wednesday night's game stream has been viewed over 14,000 times to this point. It would also be easy to say the focus should be that "this team is building on the foundation of the teams that came before" because that would also be true.

I remember winning the sectional finals against Temple Christian in a shootout my senior year (before getting beat by the Alex Hanna-led O-G Titans in the district semis). I remember watching my brothers – Devon and Adrian – when their strong teams made some noise in the tournament. I remember Jeremy Parkins and Matt Renfrow and the awesome teams they led. I remember Tristan Smucker, and the August boys, and the Reichenbach twins, and the Garrett trio, and a hundred other names I don't have the space to mention here. I remember the coaches including Dave Fett and now Steve Smucker. I also remember Bill Gaines and Dave Lee and their sons and the work they put in to build the first Pirate teams. We have Steinmetz Field, and Bluffton Soccer Club, and Citizens Fields thanks to the support – financial and otherwise – of key contributors. It would be easy to say the focus should be on the parents who deserve this because of the time (and the money, and even more time) they have invested in their sons, and that would be true. By doing a little Darryl Nester calculus (another Bluffton Pirate Superfan and father of a Pirate soccer alumnus; I did get a C+ in Calculus, by the way) I calculate that the average parent has attended more than 240 soccer games, dropped a kid at soccer practice at least 1,152 times, done 1,392 loads of soccer laundry, and been to way too many soccer tournaments in Beavercreek. But in addition to these facts and focuses, there are a few other things I love the most about this tournament run.

This team has character. I'm not sure I've ever seen a team and its players rise to the occasion like the 2019 soccer Pirates. Nic Essinger played the game of his life against Ottawa Hills in the regional final with some truly unbelievable saves in overtime and the shootout. Jonathan Schriner fought through double teams the entire tournament to score the winning goal Wednesday night against South Range. Jude Spallinger dribbled around the keeper on a breakaway to beat Fairview in the regional semifinals. The defense collectively shut the door time after time on some very talented teams. The team as a whole came from behind in multiple games to advance. Every single player – on the field and the bench – stayed on the same page and worked together no matter how much time they actually spent on the field. I really love the fans and their passion. I love the coaches and their dedication. I love the grin on Steve Smucker's face after Wednesday night's game. I love the collection of Dan Lee selfies with the team he posted on Facebook. I loved catching up with BHS alumni at the games. I loved Brandon Good in the middle of Wednesday night's enormous prayer circle after the game. I loved giving high fives to anyone and everyone - strangers included - whenever the Pirates scored a goal.

So, no matter the outcome, the Pirates and their fans have already won. And as a former Pirate athlete, and as a current Pirate coach, father, Blufftonite, and fan, I couldn't have asked for a better, more satisfying ride. And, in the words of Tyler Chamberlain, I've got my fingers crossed that on Sunday "the Slipper Still Fits!"

Bluffton's past perfect

By Fred Steiner

This chapter includes essays about Bluffton residents no longer living. Some are eulogies given at their funerals. Fred Steiner is the author of this material with the exception of the final story.

Keeper of obscure, yet significant, Bluffton footnotes

Richard "Dick" Jordan – When I think of Dick Jordan, several things come to mind. His license plate: 528 YZ. That was the family address on South Main Street. The Masonic Lodge: "A society of secrets, not a secret society," or so he claimed. His Jordan triplets: two brothers and one sister. My brother, Rudi, their contemporary, often said that Mrs. Jordan (their mother) should have been given sainthood. "She had Jordans three at one time." His chuckle, reminiscent of the late Arden Baker's. His laugh, certainly memorable to experience, perhaps even a couple notches above A.C. Burcky's. Then comes politics. The day after the 1964 Johnson landslide against Goldwater, I happened to be standing in the post office. Dick, a then-Democrat committeeman, walked in. And standing in the postal line was a Bluffton Republican committeeman. "Nice day, isn't it, —?" asked Dick. I will not provide Mr. —'s response. But the best part of Dick, the part we will miss the most, is his explanation of obscure, yet significant, Bluffton footnotes. He never explained these in a straight line from Point A to Point B. But, getting from

A to B was the most fun. I photographed a window in a Bluffton church that includes insignias of early Bluffton lodges. I asked Dick to explain these to me. His word-for-word response came after first providing the explanation of the insignias and then came his verbiage: "As a sideline, a little-noticed stained-glass window in a minor staircase in the church bears the name of the — family, of whom I am not acquainted. However, one of them, a Miss — was romantically connected to a Mr. —, uncle and probably namesake of the perhaps better-known —. According to the late Mrs. —, the family was somewhat agitated over his venture with Miss —. A distant cousin, the late lamented —, once told of his buzzing her house in his aeroplane, or possibly he was buzzing the adjacent dwelling, then occupied by the — family and in later years known as the — home."

Classic Dick Jordan. And, concerning questions I once posed to him about rumored Bluffton-KKK connections, he replied, "Perhaps we might discuss this at a Bluffton coffeehouse establishment roundtable at some point in the future." We did. I won't provide details. The chat, not hooded in secrecy, named names, which I blush to repeat. And it failed the line test from Point A to Point B. That's what made it so memorable.

He was many things, but not quarterback of the BHS football team

Written for his memorial service.

Ropp Triplett – After its inaugural season, I asked Ropp: "How many people do you think came to Bluffton to see The Gift of Giving light show?" He answered: "5,423." I asked: "How do you know?" He answered: "I counted them." I know he didn't count them. I saw the slide rule in his pocket. He created a formula to figure it out. Bluffton and the Triplett family go way back. A young Will Triplett arrived here after the Civil War. He was intrigued by the latest technology – placing images on

78

glass plates. He became Bluffton's first photographer, a position he held for a half century. A building on Main Street carries his name: "Triplett 1900." You can see it way up on the top of the building. Today it's a pharmacy. It was Will's building. Will's son, Ray, graduated from Bluffton High School. He was quarterback of Bluffton High School's first-ever football team. Ray was intrigued by the latest technology. He created a hand-held device that did lots of things. And it was in great demand. You might say he was 100 years ahead of his time. He started a small business in Bluffton creating his products. After 20 years in business his company was Bluffton's largest employer. Bluffton was a one-factory town. The business remained in the Triplett family for over three-quarters of a century. Ray's son, Ropp, graduated from Bluffton High School. He was not quarterback of the high school football team. He entered the service and afterward returned to Bluffton to work for the family business. At its height, this family business employed over 800 persons, working three shifts with property in Bluffton of over three acres. It had plants in other communities and other states. Ropp was the most important person in Bluffton. Ropp's Presbyterian buddy, Mister Eugene Benroth, posed an idea to Ropp, which would demonstrate the importance of the family business to Bluffton. It was this: Once a month Ropp should pay employees with silver dollars. As those dollars spread around Bluffton the economic impact of the company would be obvious. Eugene thought it was a great idea. Ropp thought otherwise. We just wish we had the silver dollars.

In 1965 this community experienced its most devastating natural disaster: a Palm Sunday tornado. Here are some of the facts: Nine persons killed, damage totaling over $4 million, more than 600 buildings completely destroyed in Allen and Hancock County, more than 20 families in the Bluffton school district relocated because of loss of home, 42 persons treated for injuries in one night at Bluffton Community Hospital. Ropp Triplett was named general chairperson of the relief and clean-up efforts. Those efforts involved 200,000 hours of volunteer labor, over 5,000 meals served to volunteers, nearly 300 persons clothed, and Ropp Triplett chaired the relief efforts. He was the most important person in Bluffton. Because of his position in his family business, Bluffton's largest employer, Ropp was the only person in Bluffton in his tax bracket. Yet, he chose to drive a Buick all his life. It was his "brand." The other Triplett family vehicle, a tan American-made econo van, demonstrated Ropp's efficiency. It had a hole in the floor. Ropp drilled the hole. You see, when you or my families went on vacations, we stopped at rest stops. Not the Tripletts. They didn't have to. Because of his position, much was expected of him. And he returned the expectation graciously, generously and anonymously. Because of his generosity, how many Bluffton institutions could carry Ropp's name above the entranceway? We'll never know for certain. But, for certain those could include: Bluffton Public Library, Bluffton Community Hospital, Bluffton Family Recreation, Bluffton Center for Entrepreneurs. Probably many more. And this does not include the countless small business start-ups where Ropp was the anonymous "angel" investor or generous "encourager." This encouragement includes the Bluffton Icon. The Triplett Bike Path was the one that got away. The Bluffton council did an end run around Ropp and Mary Em. The council named the bike path in their honor. Ropp would have preferred to call it simply the Bluffton Bike Path. Ropp's most recent artistic creation, The Gift of Giving light show extravaganza, is another example of Ropp from start to finish. You'd have to go to Toledo or Cincinnati to see anything like it. The Gift of Giving, to Blufftonites who knew him, reveals Ropp's philosophy. It is "the gift...of giving." Thank you, Will Triplett, for settling in Bluffton. Thank you, R.L. Triplett, for helping to make Bluffton what it is today. Thank you, William Ropp Triplett, for your continual gift of giving.

He took them on like a mongoose attacking a cobra

Phil Yost – Like most people, I believe that I will live forever. I do pause, when a classmate or personal friend proves that one doesn't live forever. It hasn't happened often, but when it does I do stop and reflect. Involving the Bluffton High School class of 1968, of which I belong, I think of Max Eastman and Rayleigh Habegger, for example. Each was a friend of mine. Each was extremely intelligent and talented. When Rayleigh died she left, I believe, two pre-teen children, who I've never met. My connection with Rayleigh started in Kindergarten. Her mother and my mother were in the same mothers' club. They probably also attended high school together. Her brother, Ron, was in my sister's high school class. So, we had much in common. Max's death struck me more deeply because we were close friends and our relationship went back to second grade, Methodist Church, midget football and several other connecting points. Now, Phil joins this list. My first-ever recollection of Phil was in the fifth grade. He lived at the north end of Spring Street and I on the corner of Lawn and Elm. We often walked home from school together. Somewhere along the line, I may have picked up the notion that he skipped a grade and was actually one of the youngest members of our class. For some reason, it was always important to know who was oldest and youngest. He was pretty proud of his age ranking. Then Phil and his family moved to mysterious Tennessee. It was a place none of us – by this point, other close friends, Rick Emmert, Jim Heiks and myself – had ever visited. It seems his dad was in divinity school, or something like that. Phil returned to Bluffton – I can't remember when. By this time sports took a back seat to academics for Phil. If I were lucky enough to sit beside him in study hall in the old auditorium, he'd fix my math problems while he did his English assignment – at the same time. I really had problems with math and could never figure out why it was so easy for him. By the time high school came around my connection with Phil was in band and choir. He played flute and was one of the most bow-legged marching band members I ever knew. Even more so than Gregg Luginbuhl, who was the king of bow-leggedness. This characteristic was never considered a flaw, simply a point of interest among our classmates.

Phil was a superb flutist. He was also an excellent singer and actor. He played old Mr. Macgregor in our high school musical "Brigadoon," when we were seniors. It was during one of the "Brigadoon" rehearsals that we learned of Martin Luther King, Jr.'s death. During the late 1960s at Bluffton High School there were few gray areas when it came to race relations. You were either for it or you were against it. Most of our attitudes came down to us from our parents. No matter, I remember a heated discussion in the old BHS gym when word trickled around about King. Lots of the "tough guys" were bragging about it. Phil took them on like a mongoose attacking a cobra. The few of us on Phil's team were very proud of him that night. One time Phil, Rick, Jim and I spent an over-nighter at Emmert's. We stayed up late into the night talking about who knows what. If you can imagine this conversation, you can envision how loud it became. Phil, Rick and Jim were not the type of young boys to be out-shouted on any subject. They knew everything about the world and needed to prove it. Of course, I was the quiet one – and didn't know everything about the world. These were friendly conversations. Not all conversations, however, were friendly. Being baptized as a baby in swaddling clothes, across Church Street in the dark brick building, I had already made it to heaven. Because of this I was told by these three guys from the church with the yellow bricks that one must be an adult to make a decision as important as the one my parents made for me. I defended the faith as well as I could, but it was always three to one. Around this time results from the various pre-college testings were made available. We learned that Phil was in the 99th percentile of nearly each test he took. This was his finest hour, at least in our eyes. He and Rick went off to Earlham. Jim and I stayed home and attended Bluffton. Our paths didn't cross much after that. However, an interesting set of circumstances occurred that bonded Phil and me. It was the Selective Service draft during the Vietnam War. Jim and Rick each had high – safe – draft numbers. Phil and I struck out with low numbers. We were going to be drafted one way or the other. We both believed we were wronged by a corrupt government. This was especially our view because Jim and Rick were safe. I watched Phil during this period, wondering what he'd do when his number was called. Some guys we knew went to Canada. Some guys we knew burned their draft cards. Some guys we knew stayed in the shadows and somehow avoided the whole mess. I really wondered what Phil would do. Honestly, he surprised me. He went to the Cincinnati inner city and served two years in a voluntary service assignment. Fate had a different plan for me. My number was 80. The draft ended at number 79. The next thing I knew Phil was working at the Middletown newspaper. Then he moved to California, continuing his career in print. Oddly I followed a similar career path, but on a much smaller scale. The years passed. We probably saw each other three times tops between the 1970s and this year.

So I ask myself: Why Max, Raleigh and Phil? Why not me? Yeah, I should have stayed in touch. We did have much in common. I should have written him a month ago. I should have called. I didn't. I should have gotten to know his wife. I should have called her. I probably still could. But, what am I going to say? I should have visited his parents. I should have called them. I probably still could. But, what am I going to say? Once upon a time, a very long time ago, Phil Yost was a good schoolmate friend. He was a well-thought-of kid. He was extremely intelligent, gifted, funny, full of talent and creative. He was argumentative to the degree that there was no point crossing him – you'd lose. He had nice parents. He came from a "good family." I guess that's how I'm going to remember Phil. I wish I could do more. But this is all I can do. I'm going to miss Phil.

For kids in our neighborhood, she was warden, ringmaster, psychiatrist and popper of popcorn

Written for her memorial service.

Alice DeVier – The DeViers and my family go way back. Way back. Alice and my mother were in the same mothers' club. Francis, her husband, and my parents went to Bluffton school together in the 1920s and 1930s. Alice and Francis' children, Jim, Val, Bonnie and Sue, had a dog named Rudy. My sister, Mary, and I have a brother named Rudi. This got pretty confusing when both families were called to come in for supper. Let me tell you about our neighborhood. DeVier's house was right in the center. Behind it lived Judy Westrick. On the north lived an older couple, Sam and Della Stepleton. Across the street lived Roger and Anita Augsburger. Our house was across from DeVier's. On the other corner of Lawn and Elm was Bill Schumacher's. It was later the home of Vickie, Robin and Penny Wilch. It was more than that. There were grandparents nearby. Judy's grandmother, Olga Amstutz, lived next to her. The DeVier kid's grandparents lived four doors up the street. My grandparents lived next door to us. Jan Benroth's grandfather lived with him. The Wilch sister's grandparents, the Kempfs, lived three doors down the street. There was still more. The DeVier's Aunt Daisy and Aunt "Tech" (for Teresa) also lived close by. I didn't know these two women had last names until I was older. The adults in our neighborhood were all children of the Great Depression. We kids knew what that meant: Don't throw anything away. Just look at the DeVier garage, the Steiner garage and the DeVier grandparents' barn. The DeVier barn was the best barn in Bluffton. It had everything a kid needed. These things included tables, chairs, unmatched table settings, bed springs and license plates. It was a perfect hideout for kids. Alice played a significant role with the kids in our neighborhood. She was a psychiatrist, banker, warden, maker of popcorn and funeral director. We buried more birds, rabbits, squirrels, dogs and cats in the DeVier and Steiner yards under her direction than I can begin to count.

Let me tell you about the DeVier backyard. It was a perfect croquet, baseball and football field. The boundary on one side was Alice's clothes line. The other boundary was the reason the kids in our neighborhood were never constipated. It was Alice and Francis' green grape arbor. We could never tell when the grapes weren't ripe. They were always green. So, we ate them all the time. Along the side of the house, in the summer, was placed the DeVier aluminum pop-up car-carrier camper, which Francis made. I can't count the times we slept out in it and had Alice's popped corn as a late-night snack. Let me tell you about the DeVier's front yard. If there was an Olympic competition for kick-the-can, our neighborhood would have been all-stars. Alice's front porch step should be a national monument to the game. It was base. There's probably a crop circle in the front lawn of the property today. It was created by the number of times we sat in the circle and played spin the bottle. And I wonder just how many Monopoly game boards we wore out. I can still see us trying to stay out beyond 8:30 p.m. while hearing Alice step out on the porch. One by one, she'd name her kids. Then she'd say the three words we all dreaded: "Time for bed."

There's another part to Alice. She played the piano. She was interested in genealogy. She was a crossword puzzle fanatic. She played that crazy word search game in The Lima News. In later years she was the next thing to a daughter to the Stepletons, as they grew older, and were unable to take care of themselves. She and Francis were square dancers. Big time square dancers. She was in the Eastern Star. She was a budgeter. Soon after Christmas one year Jim showed me all the presents he received. Then I showed him mine. "Mom said that they spent $15 on each of us this Christmas," Jim proudly announced to me. Fifteen dollar on each! I was amazed. That was a lot of money. Alice might have at one time been the fastest typist in Bluffton. She was secretary to Dr. Lloyd Ramseyer, president of Bluffton College. She was also a front desk receptionist and proofreader at the Bluffton News. Astrologically, Alice was a Scorpio. That meant that she was a very loyal person. Scorpios get along with other Scorpios. (I'm one too.) But watch out. Never step on one. If someone tried to cross Alice, beware. I took note of those who tried. Several times I've been privileged to use the Alice DeVier Method myself, when stepped upon. It works. Sometimes when I'm at my parent's house at night I look over at DeVier's and see just one light on. I think to myself that the "DeViers are asleep. It must be time for me to go to sleep, too." Looking at their house at night gives me a warm, pleasant feeling. Then I remember that it's really 2002 and DeViers don't live there anymore. It was time for Alice to go to sleep. Today we are grateful for how she contributed to our lives and how she helped make our neighborhood the interesting one that it was.

How many quilts did she create?
No one knows for certain
Written for her memorial service.

Ada Gierman – Let me tell you about my Aunt Ada Gierman. She was born 91 years ago this month on the Steiner family homestead, four miles west of Bluffton. She was in the third generation of Steiners living on the farm. Her parents and grandparents had biblical-sounding names. Her grandparents were Abraham and Mary Ann Kohler Hochstettler Steiner. Her parents were Noah F. and Susan Gerig Steiner. She was the ninth of 11 children born to Noah and Susan. Four died in infancy. There was Edna, Emma, Abraham (who died in infancy), Adella, Alma and then Jonathon, Rosella and Glen (all three died in infancy), then Ada, Nelson and Stanley. In the neighborhood were many cousins: Hochstettlers, Dillers, Lugibills, Sumneys, Rupps, Zimmermans, Basingers, Reichenbachs and Kinsingers. Aunt Ada's community was known as the Swiss Settlement. It was the farm land west of Bluffton. It stretched to about eight miles east and west and 12 miles north and south, all the way north of Pandora. English was the second language in the Settlement. German was the first. Most spoke in a Swiss dialect. Not our family, however. Ours spoke Pennsylvania Dutch. The church was a very important part of Ada and her family's life. We know it as the Defenseless Mennonite Church and the Evangelical Mennonite Church. Persons outside our family have no comprehension of the importance of this church to our lives. I'm told that every Saturday night the Steiner children polished their shoes before going to bed, in anticipation of Sunday morning. Let me tell you about the Hilty country school. It is still standing on the corner of State Route 696 and Columbus Grove Road. It had another name: the Silver Maple School. You can see it from the Steiner farm, too. Aunt Ada told me that her father, as a young school boy boasted that he jumped over the silver maple tree in the school yard. It was at the Hilty school where Ada and all her brothers and sisters first spoke English.

Let me tell you about living on the farm. Ada and her young brothers had a pet lamb, Lucy. It followed them everywhere. I wonder about the Pennsylvania Dutch phase: "Get this lamb out of the kitchen!" Here Aunt Ada developed a lifelong love for cooking, baking, canning, sewing and quilting. She learned to sew on a non-electric machine equipped with a foot pedal. How often have you gone to her house and she offered you a piece of ground cherry pie? How often have you gone to her house and you had to walk around the quilting frame, set up in the front room? How often have you gone to her house and the Bible was open on the kitchen table? As Bluffton News editor, I often go to the senior citizens center. Every Wednesday I would see Aunt Ada quilting and Uncle Karl making rugs on the loom. How many quilts did Aunt Ada create? No one knows. My Dad told me that his family very seldom bought groceries. They raised all their food. They canned it. Their basement shelves were full from the floor to the ceiling with canned food. In the fall they butchered. After the wheat harvest they took their wheat to the mill and made flour. They brought it home in 50-pound sacks. Do you ever feel guilty when buying a jar of jam at the store? After all you could have, you should have canned it yourself. Aunt Ada did some outdoor work, too. She and my Dad handled the family's six dairy cattle as they grazed along the road in the summer.

There are no grey areas with Steiners. Everything is either black or white. My Dad tried to teach Aunt Ada to drive a car. It was a 1918 Dodge. She either ran the car through the garage or into the garage. When the lesson was over, she said, "I'll never drive a car again." She didn't. After the Hilty school, she attended Bluffton High School. In her first two years she went to school with an Althaus neighbor. Then, when my Dad was a freshman and she a junior, those two hitched a horse to a buggy and rode to school. The horse's name was Dixie. They rode in all kinds of weather. I asked Dad how long it took to get to school. He couldn't remember, but said that the horse went at a "trot." I don't know what a trot pace is, but I imagine it took 15 to 20 minutes to get to school. Then you had to take the horse to the stable. I live on the town end of their route to school. Since I work uptown, I drive my daughter to school every day. At about three until eight we rush out the door and say, "Let's book it or we'll be late." That's when I often think of Dad and Ada coming into town in the horse and buggy. I wonder if they were ever late. Then I remember that they were Gerigs and Steiners. They were never late. The next year they came to town in a Model T. Aunt Ada was a member of the Bluffton High School class of 1929. Of all the over 120 graduating classes from BHS, that class had an interesting distinction. It named the Pirate as the school mascot. Aunt Ada was a modest person. She wouldn't tell a story that would make you blush. When she told a story, it was factual. She told me about her parents' wedding night. Her mother's sisters gave her some advice. It was to make certain that the lamp wick was short and that there wasn't much oil in the lamp. I don't know why Aunt Ada told me that story. I just know that it must be true. Here's another story that she told my sister. When Stanley was about to be born, her mother told her to take her little brother Nelson and go to Aunt Mary Ann's at the next farm. So, Ada took Nelson through their path in the field to Aunt Mary Ann's. When she came home she had a baby brother! She had no idea that her mother was pregnant. Or, as Aunt Ada would say, "Oh, the idea!" After high school, Aunt Ada took a bold step. She left the farm and attended nursing school… in Chicago. There she met Karl and they were married. Soon they returned to Bluffton and to the farm. She was a nurse at Bluffton Community Hospital for 29 years. We don't think of Karl and Ada as sports fans. However, they were. Their College Avenue porch swing faced Harmon Field, where the high school played football. I would often see them on warm evenings, sitting on their porch, watching the game. Do you know something? They had binoculars. I know. I often sat on their porch and watched some of the games with them. To know Uncle Karl and Aunt Ada you must remember their daughters, Miriam and Irlene. Both became nurses, like their mother. Ada and Karl outlived their daughters. It was difficult. It was difficult for them and for us all. Miriam and Irlene's death, however, did not alter Karl and Ada's faith. And we know that. Now it is Aunt Ada's turn to leave us. This morning I drove past their property on College Avenue. The house is no longer there. The library will soon expand into their property. But, their lilacs were in full bloom. That made me think if Aunt Ada. It was a peaceful feeling. We are all touched in some way or another by Aunt Ada. In our own ways we will remember this gentle aunt who was a friend to us all.

His footprints are evident in countless village projects

Wayne Matter – If anyone may be called a "Village Father," Wayne Matter deserves the title. He spent much of his adult life in the midst of Village of Bluffton activities and he celebrates his 90th birthday on April 21. His political career includes: Bluffton council member, 1960-65, Bluffton mayor, 1966-75, Bluffton village treasurer, 1976-80. Other community activities: Founding board member of Bluffton Housing Corp., past member of Bluffton Hospital board, 65-year member of Mt. Cory Lodge #418. As Bluffton grew during the 1960s today, Matter's footprints may be found on nearly every village project. When he stepped down as mayor he had served in that office longer than any previous mayor. During his council and mayoral era Bluffton's downtown experienced a rebirth as the first-ever streetscape program occurred. The village government expanded during this period with increases in the police department, fire, EMS and village services. During his years on Bluffton Housing Corp. that non-profit organization created Riley View and Vance Street apartments. In 1974 Riley View was constructed for $700,000. In 1984 Vance Street was constructed at a cost of $849,750. While treasurer of the Village of Bluffton, the village experienced its first-ever major annexation as it expanded in size by nearly 500 acres and became a village in two counties. As a member of the hospital board, Matter participated in its first-ever expansion, which totaled

$400,000. As an Emmanuel United Church of Christ member, he served several terms as deacon, elder, president of the consistory, sang in the choir and served on many various committees. These included the rebuilding of Emmanuel after the Palm Sunday tornado in 1965.

Born in Bluffton on Riley Street in 1925, he is the oldest of four children of Richard and Josephine Diemer Matter. When he was 6 months old his family moved to Ft. Wayne, Indiana, where he eventually graduated from North Side High School in 1943. He immediately left for the Marines where he was stationed in the South Pacific during World War II. After being discharged, he returned home then moved back to Bluffton in 1946, living with his uncle and aunt, Leah and Earl Matter. He obtained a job with the Farm Bureau. He met Janet Young at a square dance and they were married on May 7, 1947. They have seven children: Jane (Ron) Etter, Sara (Jack) Behnke, Mary (Dave) Fett, Susie (Jan) Gilliland, Ron (Laurie) Matter, Rick (Sherri) Matter, and Randy (Kim) Matter. Matter began work at Ex-Cell-O in July, 1955 and retired in 1984. In addition to all of the above, Wayne is a member of the Bluffton Golf Club's hole-in-one club, a distinction held by very few individuals.

He appreciated an interesting Bluffton story and understood it better than most

Gregg Luginbuhl – A coffee mug sits at my keyboard as I write this. It has Gregg Luginbuhl's artistic signature on its bottom. Perhaps you hold one, too, as you read this. Gregg was artist laureate of Bluffton. The title passed to him from his father, Darvin. Before Darvin, it belonged to John Klassen. Gregg also belongs in the same class as other former Bluffton artists Richard Minck and Paul Soldner. Today, art of these people is all around us and we are better for it. You'll find Gregg's art at Yoder Recital Hall, Memorial Field (baseball), SumiRiko

Ohio and locations around the community. (Also in your coffee cupboard, as previously mentioned.) But, for Gregg, his life was more than just art. He enjoyed sports and excelled at it.

He appreciated an interesting Bluffton story and understood it. He knew enough Swiss dialect to be dangerous, but used it sparingly. He liked to give his dogs human names. Norman, for example. He had a sense of humor. For the record, Gregg was the most bow-legged student to attend Bluffton High School in the 1960s. He left Phil Yost, his only competitor, in the dust. But, since Gregg was a popular guy lots of his younger admirers wished they were bow legged also. His was an admirable characteristic. Much has been mentioned about his art. He served on the board of Ohio Designer Craftsmen for many years and was president of the board from 1999 to 2001. He received the Lifetime Achievement Award from Ohio Designer Craftsmen in 2015. He retired in 2014 after 38 years of teaching university-level art. He was first tenured at the University of Findlay, teaching there from 1976-84, before returning to Bluffton University.

He served 30 years at Bluffton as professor of art and chair of the art department. He was named professor emeritus during commencement exercises in the spring of 2014. A little sports explanation. Gregg played basketball with the artistic ability that he threw pottery.

Point in fact: he had natural athletic ability. He could dribble a basketball in the middle of a crowd and escape with ball in hand. Try it. You'll probably fail. He didn't. Name the best BHS boys' basketball team ever − he could have started on any team. He did have a crazy streak, however. He not only played basketball. He also played football. Why? We asked. Answer − "So I can keep in shape for basketball." He also played baseball at BHS and was the most valuable player as a senior. More about Gregg: He was president of the BHS class of 1967. Homecoming kings didn't exist back then, but he'd have been a shoe-in for the title.

Concerning Swiss dialect, this sums it all up for Gregg. In 2011 we interviewed Gregg's dad, Darvin, for our book "A Good Place to Miss." The discussion centered on Bluffton in the 1930s. Darvin was getting forgetful. There was a Swiss phrase he wanted to offer, but couldn't remember it. Gregg, who sat in on the interview, immediate realized what Darvin was attempting but couldn't verbalize. In the clearest Bluffton Swiss dialect I've ever heard, Gregg offered: "Dad, don't you mean *Dash ish zum eina anderes Fogel [Vogel] singen?*" Then he chuckled. Translation, take your pick: There once was yet another bird, or, today there whistles yet another bird. This phrase means that there will soon be a change in the weather, because the bird has a different whistle, or bad weather is coming, or simply things are changing. Thanks, Gregg, for making Bluffton such an interesting place. Things in Bluffton certainly are changing, as you said. Your artistic presence helped it change for the better. I'll finish my coffee now.

He could speak every known Bluffton dialect
Written for his memorial service.
Joe Urich, Jr. – When they get around to listing the 50 most interesting people who ever lived in Bluffton Joe Urich will be on the list. He'll be on the list of the 25 most interesting people who lived in Bluffton. There's a phrase that best describes Joe's relationship to Bluffton. Joe was a-man-about-town. Whenever there was a fire, flood, parade or bank robbery, there is always a crowd of people who stand around afterward. Joe was always in that crowd. Joe could speak every known Bluffton dialect. He could speak the Low Bluffton dialect, spoken in a restaurant formerly known as Ingalls'. He could speak High Bluffton dialect, spoken in an art barn and recital hall on the other side of Spring Street. He could speak the confusing and often mispronounced First Mennonite dialect. He couldn't speak Swiss, but his wife could. But the dialect Joe could speak best was the

Harmon Field dialect. It was the language created by Howard Triplehorn, revised by Neil Schmidt, perfected by Joe Urich, and added to by athletes like Ramon Lewis, Todd Fleharty and Zac Kohli. Parenthetical to this talk, when the Bluffton News first announced the pre-sale of the Bluffton High School sports history book, who do you think was the first person to order a book? Joe Urich. Joe was Bluffton's Renaissance Man. We didn't give him enough credit for all the interests he had. He played the lead role in a community production of "Our Town." He was in the Air Force. He served on a peace mission to Central America. He owned a pizza shop on Main Street called "Joe's." He was on the library board. He was on the council. He was good enough to play football in the Mid-American Conference. I learned to know Joe when I was in high school. In the mid-1960s there were only two places for high school kids to get jobs: the swimming pool or Urich's IGA Foodliner. I was a freshman in high school and was mowing Ken Urich's lawn. Ken hired me to carry out groceries. Joe taught me. He taught me how to bag groceries, how to carry them out and how to stock shelves. He also taught me something else. He told me the most peculiar stories about every person in Bluffton. These were not usually stories that I could take home and tell my parents at the supper table. I took the more peculiar of the peculiar and told my brother, Rudi. He said that they were true. Then I asked him how he knew this. He told me that Joe Urich told him. Here's how it worked. Imagine that you are a high school boy stocking grocery shelves. Your Mr. or Mrs. Average Bluffton resident would walk down the aisle. As soon as the person left the aisle Joe would come over, lean his shoulder into you and say something like, "I'll bet you never knew this about that person…" Then he'd tell me his peculiar story, slap his hands together, laugh and walk off. One morning, about three years ago, quite by accident, the Bluffton News employees had locked ourselves out of the building. We were standing in front of the Church Street side door trying to politely work the door handle, in hopes of opening it. About that time, Joe came by mumbling in Low Bluffton, since he had been at the restaurant formerly known as Ingalls'. He asked if he could help. We said, "Yes." By the way, Joe had his own unique way of walking. His head was always straight back and his arm was cocked and it moved as he walked. He walked toward us in his walk, spied a half brick on the sidewalk, picked it up, slung it around his back smashing the window. We were stunned, but were able to get in the building. He never stopped walking. He simply slapped his hands together, laughed and left.

You all know the phrase "pushing the envelope." Joe never had to push the envelope. He was the father of pushing the envelope. I know. I looked it up in the American Dictionary of Slang. It read: Pushing The Envelope, a phrase created by Joe Urich, who lived in a small northwestern Ohio town in the mid-1950s. I want to tell you the benchmark story of all pushing the envelope stories. Joe told me this story. I was so amazed, that I went home and wrote it down. Here it is: Sometime while Dwight Eisenhower was president, the U.S. was creating the interstate highway system. Bluffton has its Route 25 bypass, which became Interstate 75, which was first two lanes then four. Then interchanges were added. Somewhere during this time, Joe decided that he wanted to be the first person to drive down the interstate. The very day that the pavement was poured was the day Joe took his ride. It was in a 1948 tan Ford (or Chevy). Joe drove past the roadblocks and onto the interstate. He discovered that the pavement was much wetter than he expected. He drove for a while and then somewhere got off. He drove the car home, parked it in his parent's garage and shut the door. Fortunately for Joe the tires were so bald that no one could trace the tread marks to his car. Unfortunately Joe didn't clean off the pavement, which had splattered all over the wheel wells and on the side of the car. Kaiser Gaiffe, the police chief, saw the car and realized what Joe had done. That's why Joe said he knew that it cost $1 million a mile to create an interstate highway. I don't want this to be the story you remember about Joe Urich. I want you to hear this story so that you'll know why Joe was one of the 25 most interesting people ever to live in Bluffton, Ohio. He will be sadly missed.

Post script: In Rudi Steiner's version of the interstate story, the car was a tan 1948 two-door Chevy or Olds. The event took place when the new stretch of 75 was opened from Bentley Road south. Joe and his buddies decided to be the first ones to drive on it, the new stretch. Joe told Rudi that it was fresher than they thought. They drove on it for about three miles and then somehow got off. They left their tire tracks in the cement but Joe's tires were so bald they couldn't get a tread mark to identify the tires. Joe made one mistake. He didn't wash his car, so Kaiser G. knew it was him because his car had dried cement splattered all over the fenders and the wheel wells.

Bluffton's motherlode

Mother's Day – It's difficult to count how many mothers have touched one's life. Go ahead. Try counting. Being Mother's Day weekend, I'll make a feeble attempt to demonstrate what I mean. My account could be the same as your account. Only the names would change. As a reference point, these illustrations are from my own youth. Although none of these women are my mother, each knew how to play the mother trump card. Each did it in a way to make her profession a noble one.

I'll start with the old Lawn Avenue-Elm Street neighborhood. Alice DeVier (mother of Sue, Bonnie, Val and Jim), was all of the following to the kids in our neighborhood: banker, therapist, tie-breaker, popcorn-maker; Sue Wilch Groves (mother of Vicky,

Robin and Penny), caretaker of an endless supply of homemade Kool Aid push-up pops; Edna Oyer, always willing to purchase those seed packets that grade school kids sold for school fund-raisers; Mabel Herr and Marjorie Basinger, made us think they were really trying to guess who we were on Halloween, even though it was pretty obvious; Pauline Augsburger (mother of Roger and Anita), allowed us to tear up her back yard as the neighborhood football field; Lois Benroth (mother of Jan), who always had a good story to tell from her work at Triplett; Mrs. Welch, the Missionary Church preacher's wife (mother of Reggie, Dick and Jim), who had the largest sandbox in North America, and allowed the neighborhood to build cities in it all summer. Treva Kinsinger (mother of Pauline, Mark, Kent and Clair), as a Cub Scout den mother, she was never paid enough for all she put up with the boys in Den 2, Troop 256.

Although they had no children of their own, grade school teachers Minerva Hilty and Meredith Stepleton qualify for this list, having handled 30 or more elementary youngsters 180 days a year from 8 to 3. Add to that list Theola Sutermeister, eighth grade language arts teacher. It took me years to figure out why First Methodist Church youth choir director Marcene Martz (mother of Janet, Barb and Jack) always let the boys leave rehearsal 10 minutes early each week. (We thought she was rewarding us.) And, First Methodist SS teacher Cleda Clements, who, although had no children of her own, gave boys model cars for Christmas presents because she worked at Crow's 5 and 10. Faery Stager, whose neighborhood grocery, now the location of Village Laundromat, allowed young boys to spend more time than necessary to choose their selection of penny and nickel candy. Jo Souder, as BHS band director, treated every band member as her own kid. (Sometimes this was not a good thing.) Elfrieda Howe, who somehow managed to turn her house into a Kindergarten five days a week. She taught us how to make turtles from those orange candies and cloves. Gerry Fields, who as the head checkout at Urich's IGA, wasn't afraid to put teenage carryout boys in their place.

If Dick Jordan was Bluffton's thesaurus, Charles Hilty was our encyclopedia

Charles Hilty – One of Bluffton's thousand points of light dimmed when Charles Hilty, a Bluffton favorite son, died of Covid-19. An earlier generation appreciated him as our own talented small-town newspaper editor, making his an important voice in our village. In 1967, he left us to eventually edit the St. Louis Post-Dispatch. And, although a Republican, he claimed that had Richard Nixon's enemy list expanded from 8 to 9, he might have been on the list. We'll never know, but it makes a great Charles Hilty story. After the Post-Dispatch era he joined the H.W. Bush administration as the Number 2 man in the United States Department of Agriculture. Pretty impressive for a guy who wasn't a Future Farmer of America while attending Bluffton High School. Add to that, we recall this comment from the late Dr. Howard Raid, who often spoke highly of him: "Charles Hilty never sat on a tractor in his life." Never mind. Two other notable small-town accomplishments are that Charles was Bluffton High School's first-ever student to receive an appointment to the U.S. Naval Academy. And, he turned it down. As an editor on a slow summer no-news-week, he published a 7-page newspaper (figure this one out for yourself). This same small-town editor reporting a Bluffton HS basketball game wrote that one Pirate "shot like a broken machine gun." The player left the team following the release of that week's copy of the Bluffton News.

To hear him tell it, his birth was an American political omen. "I was born 15 minutes before the 1934 mid-term polls opened," he once said. "My birth marked the very bottom of the Great Depression for the Republican Party." Adding that when born there were only 88 Republicans among the 432 members of Congress (48 states in 1934), representing the largest-ever congressional majority for the Democrats in U.S. history. When his father went to vote later in the day he announced that Bluffton has one more Republican. And, after leaving Bluffton for a half century, he returned to live out his final days. However, his Virginia vanity license plate reading "45817" hinted to many of us that he never really left town. Meanwhile, a bumper sticker on his Mercury read: "Bail out Studebaker." You may interpret it any way you wish.

A Bluffton encyclopedia

At his best, Charles could entertain a group with the most peculiar Bluffton stories involving long-deceased and generally forgotten folks anywhere from the Civil War era up to and including 1967, the year he left Bluffton. As Bluffton's recognized encyclopedia of people, places and things, his stories ranged from Andrew Hauenstein, Civil War veteran; Bob Lewis, long-time Bluffton barber; Eugene Benroth, man-about-town; funeral directors, mayors, police chiefs, Pirate athletes to our Main Street one-of-a-kinds. These stories made the village come alive leaving you wondering how Bluffton was gifted with more town characters per hundred than most other burgs boasting three or less stoplights on its main drag.

These "Chuck Talks," borrowing a modern phrase, rose to various crescendos when Dick Jordan, Charles's Masonic brother, himself Bluffton's thesaurus, joined the discussion. In these moments, pretty soon, as the local Swiss phrase goes according to the late Roger Diller, "everyone was laughing." Meanwhile the Jordan-Hilty duets continued claiming truths of some otherwise- forgotten town genius in as serious and dignified fashion as Richard Warren might do in passing sentence to a ne'er-do-well from his perch on the Allen County Municipal Court bench. So, just to keep Charles on target, we'd lob oddball questions his way. He's always responded with a home run. An example, in his own words, tell about an early Bluffton man, Tine McGriff. This writer by error referred to him in a conversation with Mr. H. as "Time" McGriff. Here's the response: Tine McGriff....not TIME McGriff. This seems to be a common error that was made in the spelling of his name by those who didn't know him and who weren't accustomed to hearing it spoke. Hence, the error. I've always thought that Tine McGriff was a barber perhaps snipping away in the room later occupied by Bob Lewis and his various successors in that basement shop on North Main. Perhaps he once owned that building block that extended down Vine Street to include the last hangout of Dick Boehr, but I don't know.

In any case, A.G. Kibler owned the clothing and shoe store that eventually moved to the Bluffton News building, probably the room at 103 N. Main, where I apprenticed under Milton I. Edwards. The Kibler store was moved once, perhaps twice. Maybe it just moved next door, from 103 to 101 N. Main, which was Staater's clothing, dry goods and somewhat of a general store by World War I, where my mom began her career. This room later became Pete Gratz's similar store, probably in the 1920s or early '30s. I can't recall what sort of store was in that location in the late 1940s or early 1950s. I think that Kibler's – no longer A.G. Kibler – had the shop down by the "new" post office about 1946 that later became Vida's, then the Vida-Vidella Shop. By the late 1940s, early 1950s, that room at 101 had become Rice's Dry Goods and Tot Shop. Ed Rice, married I believe Ethelyn Oyer. He was a village councilman elected in 1955 (my first election, my dad's last). Not long after that, Ed Rice decamped for Medina to become the rural mail route carrier (Medina's Woody Little).

After being Rice's, 101 became Reistman's, then perhaps something else (by then I was working in St. Louis or Washington). Eventually it became the second room for the only newspaper published in town and mailed through the Bluffton post office under the favorable terms of the Postal Act of 1879.

Suddenly switching subjects to the local Swiss dialect, he continued: The resistance to German speaking in the Bluffton area, at least, began at the start of World War I. My mother, a BHS grad of 1916, studied German through much of high school, but she already spoke the Schweitzer Deutsch dialect that her parents, Swiss natives, spoke in the home. On the other hand, my dad was the only person in his class at Pandora High School who spoke only English, although quite a few were somewhat bilingual. He was chastised and derided for not speaking German when he was enrolled in a German class when a freshman at Pandora High School in 1910 or 1911. He responded by throwing his German textbook at his teacher, Wilhelm Amstutz, and leaving the class forever.

Switching these again, he continued reporting on who lived where on Main Street in the 1930s-40s-50s: The Kenny Jackson name is familiar, through word of mouth from my mother. I recall vaguely remembering a family with that name, and even more vaguely think it may have been connected to the William Jackson family on South Main Street, the home directly across the street from the former Soash house that Carole and I bought in 1965.

In the line of succession moving down that side of South Main Street there would have been, in my childhood, first, the Dan Triplehorn house and the William Jackson house. This William Jackson would have been the founder-owner of the Jackson Foundry that stood on the pointed lot at the intersection of South Jackson Street and Grove Street. The building was still standing when my childhood memories were being formed (1939-1945). I know it wasn't operating by the time that I began the paper route that I inherited from John Bauman in 1946. It was demolished in early 1946. The handsome small brick house on that small lot was built for U.S. Amstutz, an aged Richland Township landowner, who moved back to Bluffton from Nebraska in 1946. He owned the big farm west of Bluffton along the Grove Road east of the

Ebenezer church. In 1946 and afterwards it was farmed for him by the Schmutz family who he had moved east from Nebraska to farm the land.

Another John Dillinger reference

Often Charles' sermons carried three-point messages usually concluding with a John Dillinger reference. Here's one of those short subjects: A story told to me by my father was that a small, mysterious business was opened in that room (reference to the rear of 101 N. Main St.) by a guy from out of town not long before the Dillinger gang came to town. And the little business was closed and the mysterious man went away almost immediately after the bank robbery. This was told to John Bauman and me by my Dad one Sunday night in 1948 when he was driving us back from Cincinnati after taking John and me to a Reds doubleheader. My Dad and my Uncle George Kempf were both on the jury in 1934 that convicted Pierpont and other Dillinger gang members of the murder of Allen County Sheriff Jess Sarber. *(Readers might cross-reference this with the Charles Triplehorn Dillinger story on page 62.)*

The professional writing skill of Charles Hilty becomes clear in the next two stories. The first, writing about the 1965 Bluffton tornado while experiencing it firsthand, is his description of that event, written on a manual typewriter under the pressure of a deadline, during his era as Bluffton News editor:

What is a tornado?

A tornado, says the encyclopedia, is an atmospheric disturbance caused by an upward current in the warm air. As the current rises a rotary movement is caused by the inrush of cold air from surrounding areas. The velocity of the whirling movements reaches 400 to 500 miles per hour.

But a tornado is more than this. It lives and breathes and talks and has character.

A tornado is a thin old man crying thick tears and saying, "Why can't I die now?"

A tornado is a barefoot little girl clad in a ripped dress, mud spattered from ankle to eyebrow, whimpering in a hospital corridor.

It is a steer, bawling discordantly in the middle of what was a normal country road two minutes ago.

It is straw with the strength of steel, and steel with the strength of straw.

A tornado is preachers being nurses, nurses being doctors, doctors being preachers, all with the help of suddenly-kind men who are none of these things.

It is an imp, which destroys the church and spares the nearby junkyard... an imp, which blows away a fireplace, but leaves the woodpile neatly stacked.

A tornado is peace and quiet, coming with the speed and power and clamor of a thousand freight trains.

A tornado is forever.

This same small-town editor took extra time to describe a rural orchard fire. This account, from the Bluffton News, resulted in words from the orchard owner much more heated than the flames in the actual blaze. The story, written with accuracy, brevity and clarity, took a simple police report about the fifth time a fire occurred in rural Bluffton over a span of 10 springs:

The annual — trash fire was held at 4:40 p.m. Friday in the family orchard west of Bluffton on Lugabill road. The party, according to an established tradition, was not announced in advance, and the guests were summoned by the sounding of the Bluffton fire siren. In attendance were Bluffton volunteer firemen, members of the family, and several curious townspeople. Neighboring farmers, who have become accustomed to the fires generally ignored the event and went on working in their fields. It was the fifth time the — have entertained the Bluffton firemen with a grass fire in their orchard. Similar parties were held February 7, 1953, November 11, 1953, February 7, 1956 and March 28, 1962. The parties have generally been held on windy days following a spell of dry weather. Announcement of the surprise party has always come shortly after members of the family have begun burning trash in their incinerator in the center of the orchards. Arrangements for this year's fire were made by the — who was charged with burning family trash last Friday. Mr. —, who was surprised himself Friday when he reached home and discovered this orchard blaze, said he planned to speak with his — about the manner in which this year's party was arranged. Bluffton firemen noted that the orchard is now considerably smaller than it was when the first trash fire was held there in 1953, and said it is possible that this traditional fire cannot be continued very many more times.

Hosni Mubarak, president of Egypt and King Hussein of Jordan

And, this is the same small-town editor, who in 1989 sat with American diplomats in the office of Hosni Mubarak, the president of Egypt. Four days earlier he was part of a codel (congressional delegation visit) to Jordan and met King Hussein, also in a private session. Charles was the staff organizer of the visit, responsible for selecting and arranging for ceremonial gifts. The gifts were limited 50-copy printings of a book on the history of aviation, bound in fabric from the original Wright brother's plane. Here's an account of that meeting, as he showed a photo of the group.

You recognize the younger me at the left end of the low table. Left to right Rep. Wally Herger (R-California), Rep. Robert Smith (R-Oregon) and Rep. Edward R. Madigan (R-Illinois), for whom I'd left newspapering to become his senior staff member in the House. The strong jovial sinister-looking man at the other end of the table was Hosni Mubarak, the president of Egypt. This photo was taken in January of 1989, one week before the inauguration of George H.W. Bush. We are in the inner, private reception lounge of President Mubarak's office suite. Pretty big and grand for a private reception lounge. Now, where does Dr. Von Hardesty, ex-tenured history professor at Bluffton College come in? Longer part of a short story.

Background: the three Congressmen were on a codel to Jordan and Egypt in January 1989. We had met King Hussein in Jordan four days before in a similar, small private session. It is customary that a codel is to have a private visit with a head of state, to present a formal ceremonial gift to our host. As staff organizer of the visit, I was responsible for selecting and arranging for the ceremonial gifts. I knew that both Hussein and Mubarak were first-rate pilots, and deep lovers of planes and flight history. Mubarak was an ace fighter pilot before entering politics: Hussein was a qualified 747 jet pilot, and often flew his own private 747 as relief pilot to his personal command pilot on longer flights. It was also customary that when the senior American delegation leader hands the ceremonial gift to a king or president, the king or president accepts it formally and then immediately passes it to a personal aide who is standing right behind him to receive the gift. It's considered unseemly for a head of state to seem to be so eager to see the gift that he would actually open the package and look at the gift. I had asked Dr. Hardesty, then a senior curator at the Air and Space Museum, to help find a suitable gift from the museum. He produced a presentation copy of the museum's freshly published "History of Flight," autographed by the author, his boss. Furthermore, and most important, these two were of the 50 copies that had been specially bound in the remaining handsome, heavy fabric that had been left over from its recently completed restoration of the original Wright Flyer before the Flyer was rehung in an open museum gallery. Plenty of history, plenty of prestige here. Remember now, that heads of state don't open such gifts. When we'd made the same presentation to the King a couple of days before, he was very reluctant to turn loose of the package. Ed Madigan had already told him what it was. I have, even after 27 years, a strong vision of the King holding tightly to his book while a senior staff member has reached beside him to take the book away. The King holds it more tightly, the aide tugs more firmly, and a little tugging match ensues before the book is taken away before the King can open the package. Three or four days later, we have a private visit to meet President Mubarak and present "the" book. He hears the story, begins a big smile, his aide reaches forward to take the book and carry it away. Mubarak won't release it, rips off the wrapping paper and begins, with great delight, to examine the book, almost page by page. Our meeting was extended a little bit, he was even more welcoming and happy. Ceremonial gift presentations are always stiff, cool and formal... but not these two. The King didn't want to give up his book, and President Mubarak wouldn't give his up. He had to rip it open and start skimming the book. Nothing stiff and formal about these. But two guys from Bluffton, Dr. Hardesty and me had the central roles in making it happen, and I even was there for both of these moments. Don't know where these fit in your own official Bluffton archives, but there's got to be an unusually high classification for them, for Von and for me.

In 2002 John Wagner of the Bluffton American Legion Post invited Charles to speak at that year's Bluffton Memorial Day service. Due to a conflict, which will become evident, he declined, but was invited and accepted to speak the next year, which he did. Here is his response to Wagner's invitation, with the reason he was unable to attend in 2002:

"I'm honored to have such an invitation from Post 382. My dad was a member of the post, and I still have warm and vivid memories of the graveside salute ceremonies that the post provided at his burial in Maple Grove in January 1956. Although I cannot be with you this year to be your speaker, I will consider myself as Bluffton's representative to the national ceremonies being held in Arlington National Cemetery that morning. It will be my second chance to actually sit in the Amphitheatre for those ceremonies. I will be part of a small group that will lay an additional honors wreath at the Tomb of the Unknowns in special ceremonies following immediately the main ceremony. I am part of a group invited by the Pentagon to present a wreath honoring the thousands of American civilians and soldiers and sailors who were in prisons of the Japanese in the Philippines from the late 1941 to early 1945. I will think of Bluffton and of Post 382 on Memorial Day this year and I will be honored if the leaders of the post were to consider me again in 2003 or 2004.

With respect for services that members of 382 have performed for the country and for our home community, and with humble gratitude for the offer to speak at such an important ceremony.

Note: Charles' wife, Carole, as a youngster, was a prisoner of war captured by the Japanese in the Philippines in World War II, as her parents were American missionaries there.

During one of many conversations about the unusual, often misunderstood stable geniuses of forgotten Bluffton, Mr. Hilty and this writer jokingly compiled a list of the 50 most interesting people who ever lived here. You may now see why Charles Hilty is on that list... in my opinion.

About that guy from a place called Zelienople

Don Schweingruber – How can a guy from a place called Zelienople have so many friends in a place called Bluffton? That guy, let's call him "The Donald" – he would have thought it funny – showed up here about the time Nixon was in the White House. He never left. Imagine – he was hired to serve as the disciplinarian to rowdy Bluffton College students. A thankless job. But somebody had to do it. Enrollment exploded once the institution implemented his many plans. And the Schweingruber era exceeded the tenure of maybe four Bluffton College/University presidents and even more Bluffton school superintendents, police chiefs and mayors. In between handling student bad guys (and girls), he taught a Sunday school class in the English Lutheran Church to folks his parents' age. He also parented three of the wildest kids ever to graduate from Bluffton High School. Point in fact: One spray-painted a cutout image of a runner on the southwest corner of the Jackson-College intersection. Meanwhile, his wife, "Nanc," ran for school board and by our count was only the second woman to win such a seat. He never allowed us to refer to Mrs. S as "Nanc," insisting we call her by her Christian name: Nancy. And we did.

Don was all business. He never took his staff to Arby's on a weekly basis. Never posted photos of hundreds of students in his office. Never allowed students to pull fire alarms in dorms after midnight and get away with it. Never allowed his staff to have dress down Fridays. Some whispered he loved the Pittsburgh Pirates more than our own beloved Bluffton Pirates. Was it his harsh western Pennsylvania drawl? His charming, sarcastic, intellectual wit? His spartan Lutheran upbringing? His 6-4 stature? How did he become everybody's friend? It was simply this: Don built relationships with the people in his life. He was a good listener and offered thoughtful encouragement and advice. He was respected for his faith, integrity, kindness, intelligence and sense of humor. He shaped the lives of countless Bluffton students, co-workers, family members, friends, and other people in his life. Earlier this year, Bluffton University installed a bench in Don's honor inscribed with his motto: "It's all about relationships." Don, you weren't 6-4, but we stood in your tall shadow marveling at the things you accomplished. Thanks for "friending" us. We will have a conversation or two, or three on your campus bench. After all, that's the way you wanted it.

The turned-up collar was her signature look

Rudi Steiner wrote the follow letter to Stephanie Taubert, daughter of Jackie Tschantz, a classmate of Rudi's, and member of the Bluffton High School class of 1961, upon the death of Jackie. Stephanie had asked members of the class for any memories they could share about her mother. This essay responds to her request.

Stephanie:

Some time ago you asked me to share stories of your mother, Jackie Tschantz. You asked about her interests and what she was like as a teen growing up in Bluffton. I have tried to accurately portray the uniqueness of her personality as I remember her. Since you are not a Bluffton native, I thought that to understand your mom I would include some memories of your Tschantz family. My cousin in Switzerland is our family genealogist; I asked him about your Tschantz family name. He said the Tschantz name is a common in Switzerland. The Tschantz family name is recorded as early as 1412 as residents of the town of Bern. There are also Tschantz residents in the villages of Signau and Sigriswil in Canton Bern, District Emmental. My Althaus family is from a farm called "Tachaggligen" at Bretzwil, Canton Basel Landschaft, which is up the road and a couple of big mountains away from Bern. I don't know if the Tschantz family and the Althaus family knew each other before they immigrated from Switzerland, but in Bluffton our families knew each other well. So well, that the Althaus family's cow and the Tschantz family's cow shared the same pasture, which is today the field behind Marbeck Center. Our immigrant great-grandfathers attended the same German Reformed church. My mother and your grandfather Fred Tschantz were high school friends and their friendship continued throughout their adult lives. There have always been more Republicans in Bluffton than Democrats. My immediate family, the Hahns and Steiners were staunch Democrats and so were the Tschantzs. My family and your family were sometimes in the minority and opposed more popular views held by the rest of the community. We were known as "liberals" and often too progressive for others in Bluffton. I recall our families were among a very small group who in 1960 supported the candidacy of John F. Kennedy. Your mother, Jackie, was outspoken in her support for Kennedy. She plastered JFK stickers and pictures all over the front of her locker. The high school principal, Mr. Schmunk, made her remove the stickers, so she put them all over the inside of her locker, which ended up becoming a shrine to JFK and Jackie Kennedy. In a mock presidential election at Bluffton High School she was the leader of the few of us who were Kennedy supporters ... we lost. My mother, Margaret Hahn Steiner, my grandmother Bertha Althaus

Hahn, and your grandfather, were active in Democratic politics in the village of Bluffton, serving as election judges and voting election officials. As you probably remember your grandfather Fred Tschantz, a Democrat, was on the Bluffton council and served as mayor of Bluffton from 1980 until 1983. Your grandfather was a strong supporter of labor unions. In 1957 he and my uncles, who were Westinghouse employees, helped to form a labor union for a new Lima newspaper the Lima Citizen. I think your grandfather Tschantz at that time worked for the Lima News and was one of the striking workers who formed the new Lima Citizen newspaper. This was a contentious time for unions in Ohio. People were amazed that the mild-mannered Fred Tschantz could be so adamant and persistent in his support for workers' rights. Our family canceled our subscription to the Lima News in support of the striking workers. At that time in Bluffton one knew who was a Democrat and who was a Republican by which Lima newspaper was on their doorstep.

I didn't know your mom as a child growing up on North Main Street. Lawn Avenue had its own group of neighborhood kids: Sue, Bonnie and Valerie DeVier, Jan Benroth, the Welch boys and the Steinman girls, Jane and Linda. Jackie was part of the Riley Street neighborhood, which was a much larger group of kids than ours. They were made up of kids from two different Swank families, Nancy, Linda and Bill and their cousins Lynn, Jim, Shirley and Sue. The Eddys, Bonnie, Jim and Sandy, lived between the two Swank families. Across Main Street were the Mummas, the Dillmans, Sharon Steiner and Gene Matheson. The Jordan clan, Sally, Jim and the triplets Walt, Carol and Charles (who were our classmates) lived at the other end of Riley Street and I think they mingled among both groups. The families on Riley were a very closely knit group, so as a child your mom had as many friends her own age to play with. Bluffton has always been proud of its school system, which has always been recognized for excellence in educating children. However, individuality was not encouraged in the 1950s. We were taught to conform to rules and structure. Classroom seating arrangements, locker assignments, standing in line, were always done in alphabetical order. I met your mom in the first grade. Since I was an "S" and she a "T," we were destined to be around each other for the next 12 years of our education. Your mom was one of the first classmates I saw in the morning and probably the last one I saw at the end of the school day. She sat near me in most of my classes and she got us both kicked out of study hall several times for "talking." We were both "talkers" and probably shouldn't have been placed anywhere near each other.

Your mom was a child of the Fifties. She was a first generation "teenager." The word teenager was coined by our generation. She loved to dance and attended all the sock hops in the old Bluffton High School gym. Jackie knew all the latest dances and wasn't afraid to get everyone to try a new one. Like many Bluffton teens, she rushed home after school to watch Dick Clark and American Bandstand. From watching American Bandstand, Jackie expressed herself in her fashion and style. She had a classic 1950s look, which included black and white saddle shoes, bobby socks, a tight skirt and a fashionable blouse with a big turned-up collar. The turned-up collar was her signature look. I've attached a picture of Jackie by a jukebox and as you can see her collar is turn up. During our junior year, Jackie, Linda Sommer, Billy Steiner and I were chemistry lab partners. Chemistry was not our best subject. We didn't blow up the chemistry department, but your mom successfully set off the biggest volcano eruption ever made in a BHS chemistry lab. I guess it was the sulphur she added to the concoction that stunk up the basement of the high school for three days. Students who were unaware of the active volcano eruption thought the girl's bathroom had a sewer backup. That's how bad she stunk up the place. I remember she enjoyed reading novels. Instead of studying in the study hall, Jackie usually had her head in a novel. Two books she read that I remember were

Harper Lee's book "To Kill a Mockingbird" and for some reason she identified with the character Boo Radley. The other book was "Lolita." That's the one she let me read all the good parts. After Friday night football and basketball games Bluffton High School teens headed to Al Ingalls' Pine Restaurant to hang out. Al had a Seeburg jukebox that played all the latest hits we heard on Top 40 radio stations. The jukebox gave you five plays for a quarter. Jackie loved a doo wop group called The Diamonds. At Al's, new hits were added weekly, and one night to her surprise a new song by The Diamonds was on the jukebox. Jackie put her quarter in the jukebox and selected the new song to play five times; for some reason the mechanical Seeburg got stuck on Jackie's quarter. To her delight and to the dismay of others, The Diamonds' song "She Say" (Oom Dooby Doom) was the only song that jukebox played that Friday night. I suggest you listen to "She Say" on YouTube to capture the feeling and emotions of why she liked The Diamonds. Maybe you'll hear what she heard in this classic 1950s doo wop song. On Friday night Jan. 30, 1959, Jackie went to a basketball game in the old high school gym, and sat with the clique of girls she usually hung out with. It was really cold and snowing that night, in fact the snow continued all that weekend and into the next week. That night Bluffton defeated Columbus Grove 48 to 43. About 9:45 p.m. after the game was over, she walked into the Pine Restaurant with her friends. She ordered her usual: a hamburger, French fries and a Coke, she put a quarter in the jukebox and played her favorite songs. About 11 p.m. everyone left Al's, since we were expected to be home by 11:30. I know this is true because I was there that night. The following Wednesday our pop culture world changed by the tragic deaths of Buddy Holly, "The Big Bopper" and Ritchie Valens who died when their plane crashed in a snowy field in Iowa. These were the first of our teen idols of the 1950s to die tragic deaths. Feb. 3, 1959, has been referred to in popular culture as "the day the music died."

At times Jackie could be weird. She had some quirks. In our junior year we got our class rings. On the face of the ring was our graduating year, "1961." Jackie discovered that upside down "1961" was the same as right side up. This drove her nuts. She thought there had to be a name for this phenomenon. For weeks she searched for the answer. One of our classmate's dad was a college math professor. It was from Dr. Shetler that she got her answer. One morning she was all excited when she announced to everyone the she had found the answer to the "1961" upside down dilemma. It was called a strobogrammatic number. Then she mumbled, "Now all I have to do is learn how to pronounce it." Her quirkiness moved on to palindromes after she discovered "A man a plan a canal Panama" is a phrase that reads the same forward or backward. Jackie enjoyed acting. She had major roles in both our junior and senior class plays. She loved being on stage. Victor Borge was a popular pianist, composer and comedian in the 1950s. As a comedian he was famous for reading passages from literature by exaggerating sentence punctuations phonetically. In our freshman English class Jackie performed before the class by reading several parts from Macbeth using Victor Borge phonetic punctuation. Using her mouth, Jackie made sounds with accompanied hand gestures for commas, periods, question marks and exclamation marks. It was hilarious, and word spread about how good she performed her comedy act. Jackie performed her rendition of Shakespeare's Macbeth for all English classes that day.

Jackie was always popular and a lot of fun to be around. She participated in all school functions. She was someone you could count on to decorate the gym for a sock hop, bake a cake for a bake sale or clean up after a class social activity. I don't member when I saw Jackie last. Life after high school sent us down separate paths that never seemed to cross again. After college I came to Chicago and have been here ever since. I heard she went to California. There are certain people you meet in life that stick with you forever. Your mom was one of those people. Maybe it was her lipstick that always seemed way too bright. Maybe it was that turned-up collar or that stupid doo wop song. To this day when I smell sulphur, I think of the expression on her face when her volcano erupted. I still celebrate the day the music died. It always seems to be cold and snowing on Feb. 3.

Bluffton University is built on the pasture where the Tschantz and Althaus cows once roamed. The old high school gym is still there but they don't hold sock hops or basketball games there anymore. You can't put a quarter in a jukebox and play a 45 record at Al Ingalls' Pine Restaurant. It closed 50 years ago. Today music somehow magically appears in my iPhone. I don't know how it gets there, it just happens. Things change – I like change, when it's for the good. Life changes constantly, our loved ones die, but we never forget them. Their legacy and our memories of them live on forever. Thank you for asking me to share my memories about you mom, Jackie Tschantz.

Bluffton askew

The following essays are portions of "15 minute" interviews posted on the Bluffton Icon over the past 10 years and columns written about Bluffton residents who made our town so interesting. The question and answer format from the interviews is removed, thus resulting in some essays becoming a bit disjointed, but the reader gets the idea. One exception involves rules on pruning fruit trees. It fits this chapter because it is truly askew.

Blaming it on Becky Reineke Boblitt

Interview with Megan Weisenbarger Gustitis – I blame this all on Becky Reineke Boblitt. She convinced me to go out for the eighth grade team. Let me be blunt, this was not a good fit. Forget the fact that I could barely run up and down the court in those old, moldy gyms without stopping for a puff on my inhaler, I also had a limited sense of the rules, no shot, poor understanding of the plays, and zero inherent skill. But Becky and the other girls, Missy Pearch Moskau, Janis Badertscher, Angie Klausing Hartman, Christa Badertscher Woolum – also basketball stars – and Coach Cindy Badertscher Lee, never made me feel bad, and just kept putting me out there to play. In fact, there was one game that we were winning by some unbelievable margin. Seriously, 86-6, or something. Throughout the entire fourth quarter the Lady Pirates ran one play. I was to get to the top of the key, someone would pass me the ball, and I would try – try is the optimal word here – to shoot a basket. I missed, I missed again. I kept missing. Then, by the grace of God, one ball fell through the hoop. Both sides of the stands, filled with parents and friends of two small towns stood and screamed their heads off when this awkward preteen finally produced two points. I think I scored one more basket that year, and Becky tried her best to encourage me to continue on with the team into high school. I made it to the first day of open gym in 9th grade... and never stepped foot on that court again except to cheer on that great team of girls with my piccolo in the pep band.

While basketball didn't work out, BFR soccer was something that I loved. Dave Lee and Mustaq Ahmed were my coaches growing up. What patience. When we had outgrown the rec league, a bunch of us still wanted to play, but this was right before girls' teams were being formed in the local schools. We convinced Tim Barhorst to coach an all-girls team and we named ourselves the Bluffton Brutes. There weren't very many other girls' teams in our age group, so we ended up playing against a number of high school-aged boys' teams. We didn't care. We really wanted to show them we could play just as hard as them. I think that need to prove ourselves drove us harder than anything else. In terms of music and clubs, I think I tried everything. I played piano, cello, bassoon, drums, flute/piccolo in the bands and orchestra. I was involved in student government, the theater productions, the yearbook and the quiz bowl team. As I always tell people who are not from Bluffton, with a school this size, everyone had to participate if anything was going to happen. They never believe me when I tell them that the cheerleaders who played an instrument marched with the band at halftime, and that the biggest, baddest linemen on the football team also had lead roles in the school musical.

Let me tell you about my dad (Phil Weisenbarger) playing Santa Claus. He would get up on our house roof every Christmas

Eve regardless of the weather. Ask him about the year there was an ice storm and he talked to us through my bedroom window. One year, he dragged my brother up there with a red-filtered flash light and told him to flash it on and off like Rudolph. It was super special, and it took me a long time to figure out why Dad always missed Santa's visit. One more thing. I took my driver's test in my grandmother Weisenbarger's Dodge 600. My mom took Jannie Barhorst and I over to complete the test. Jannie had been practicing in my car because she usually drove a truck and didn't think it would be a great idea to take the test in a pick-up. I aced the driving part, and epically failed the maneuverability portion. The instructor had to dig a cone out from underneath the car. Jannie passed both. In my car. It was a long ride home.

Paddled in high school and participated in a history-making Panama flyover

Interview with Ron Edinger – I grew up in the second house from the county line on Main Street. My brothers are Jim, Jerry and Dick. I was just another face in the crowd at Bluffton High School. I played baseball and for one season, football. I was paddled following a high school assembly, either as a sophomore or junior. Actually, the entire row was paddled. The assembly featured a speaker who encouraged participation from the students. He asked us to clap our hands and the row I happen to sit in must have over-done it. We were stomping our feet. I was sitting in the wrong row. *(Fact check with Rudi Steiner, BHS class of 1961: "This paddling incident did take place. I was in the same assembly.")* I attended Bluffton College one year and transferred to the OSU branch in Lima and finished in a five-year engineering program at OSU in Columbus. I became a math teacher at Miami East High School in 1965.

I really wanted to see the world, however. I met a military recruiter and I wanted some adventure in my life. I wanted to get into flight training and I did. I had six months of training in an F4 Phantom and eventually flew 192 combat missions in southeast Asia from November 1969 to November 1970. After that I applied to the FBI and was accepted to the academy, but didn't end up going there. (Long story). Then I became a postal inspector in New York City, but decided that New York living wasn't for me. So, I met another Air Force recruiter and joined the Air Force Reserve. I flew C-123Ks a couple of years. I moved to Ft. Walton Beach and worked as a civil engineer, but continued in the Reserve. I flew to Panama in what I thought was a training exercise and ended up participating in the overthrow of Manuel Noriega. In 1991 I was on-call for Desert Storm. I retired in 1994 as a USAF Reserve Colonel. The Reserve and Guard are very demanding positions. You may keep a regular job and I did as an electrical engineer at Elgin Air Force Base in Florida. I retired from there after 10 years, in 2004. I flew 4,500 hours, which included 400 combat hours. Let's see, I was in Germany Italy, Egypt, Saudi Arabia, Mexico, Panama, Columbia, Peru, Hong Kong, Japan, Thailand, Laos, Vietnam, Guam, the Philippines, and Midway. Probably missed some. I've been in all 50 states. I was in Iran before the Shah fell. And, one of the strangest things I witnessed was a World War II Japanese destroyer docked at Midway in 1973. I've learned a lot about other cultures. Yes, I've seen the world.

I can also tell you that during school I worked at Jorg Hatchery. I couldn't eat chickens for years after that. And, I almost drowned in the quarry. Seriously. I signed up for swimming lessons and ended up in a class with swimmers much more advanced than I was. The instructor told us to swim across the Buckeye. Everybody did but me. I was exhausted soon after I started. That was my last swim lesson.

A walkie-talkie at the state track meet

Interview with Roger Triplett – The most memorable, in fact, and only memory I have, from Kindergarten was the morning I arrived to find that the classroom door was already closed. This obviously meant that I could not go in and maybe even meant that school had been cancelled, so I headed home. While walking away from school, a passing motorist noticed me, rolled down their window, and called me by name. I ran to the nearest hedgerow and hid in the bushes, until the person retrieved me and returned me back to Kindergarten. The rest of the day and the rest of the school year have all been forgotten. Do you remember the time that our sixth grade teacher informed the class that batteries did not have electricity? Of course, I had to set the record straight. However, that level of talking back to the teacher resulted in a severe and painful ear twisting. It only took a second occurrence for me to learn that you never, ever, talk back to a teacher. I objected to the lesson informing us that the earth was capable of producing its own light, called "earth shine." Wow, did my ear really hurt that time, but never again.

My first competition at the state track meet, during my junior year, was a comedy of mistakes. Everything went wrong from getting lost on the way, arriving late, and then finding out that my "technical advisor," brother Larry, was not allowed to be near the competition. It was a fantastic learning experience that prepared me for my senior year. We arrived early and were equipped with walkie talkies. Communications with my technical advisor, who was seated in the grand stand, went flawlessly. We discussed and reviewed each jump, making the necessary adjustments to compensate for the swirling winds within the OSU horseshoe stadium. So you tell me, was it preparation, experience, and training that enabled a second place finish or did I get an advantage by saving the energy that would have been required to consult the coaches in the bleachers?

Let me tell you how fun it was to live in a family – Greg, Larry and Bill – with such creative brothers as I had. We created a UFO that was actually a lightweight plastic bag we got from the dry cleaner, with a set of candles to make it a hot air balloon. It was released to fly free, at night. Of course the wind direction took it directly over a neighbor's house, who truly believed in UFOs. I am surprised the U.S. government was not summoned to investigate. My first computer was an Apple IIe, which I bought in the early 1980s. If you remember this model of computer, everything had to be entered by typing on the keyboard. A few years before I bought my own computer I was able to use the world's first personal computer, the Xerox Alto. It had a mouse, graphical user interface, and internet connectivity. It is amazing to see how Xerox computer technology has become the standard for the world. I chose the photographic engineer program at Rochester Institute of Technology (RIT) because of my strong interest in photography and in math and science. RIT also was home of the National Technical Institute for the Deaf, which is why I ended up living in a dormitory for the deaf. Yes, some of the alarm clocks and door bells were very interesting, ranging from vibration to strobe lights. When the fire alarm went off, the dorm would light up like a Christmas tree, and you could see it from miles away. There were many false alarms during the night, triggered by students who wanted to see the light display. Oh yes, I did learn basic sign language.

It was as if the whole of Bluffton's life history flashed before me

Column on the Bluffton HS class of 2004 commencement – I couldn't help myself. It was both the pomp and the circumstance of the situation on Saturday night. There I sat with hundreds of others, watching the 123rd Bluffton High School graduating class march down the aisle. My mind hit the proverbial genealogical

Bluffton black hole as the class members marched. Suddenly it was if the whole of Bluffton's life history flashed before me. The number of three- and four-generation students whose family members attended Bluffton schools jumped out at me like a sideline crowd at a BHS-Grove football game. They each appeared before me in a sort of jumbled-up mist. As a disclaimer, I've certainly missed someone or failed to relate it correctly. My apologies. First came Matt Diller. His father, Larry, was in the class of 1972. Larry's father, Cleo, was in the class of 1950. Cleo's father, Harley, attended Diller country school (somewhere on the Bluffton-Pandora school district line), and Harley's wife, Alma, graduated from BHS in 1921. Then came Allee Gratz-Collier. Her mother, Carolyn, graduated from BHS in 1973. Carolyn's father, Delbert, graduated in the 1930s. Delbert's mother, Fanny Lauby, graduated in 1914. Julianne Niswander was next. Her father, Ned, graduated in 1972. Ned's mother, Alice, graduated sometime in the 1940s. Alice's mother, Adella, graduated in the early 1920s. On a stretch, Julianne can go five generations. Adella's father, Noah Steiner, attended the Hilty school. Then came my own daughter, Anne. She can count me, as a 1968 grad, her mother, Mary, a 1974 grad, and her grandparents Margaret Steiner, BHS 1931, and Nelson, BHS 1929. On another stretch, she can claim the same Noah Steiner who Julianne Niswander claims. Anne's great-grandfather is Noah, who attended Hilty school. About this time things got really interesting. I spied Don Herr in the visitors' bleachers. He has two grandchildren, Amber Herr (daughter of Jim) and Brad Numbers (son of Susie) in the '04 class. Jim and Susie are BHS grads, as is Don, who proudly proclaims he was class president of the 1949 class. His father, Edgar, graduated in 1918. Tyler Hochstettler's mother, Chris, graduated from BHS. Her father, Keith Brauen, graduated in the class of 1947. Keith's father, Dennis, graduated in the early 1920s, perhaps 1922.

Another grandfather of two grads is Lynn Carmack. He sat in the home bleachers. His granddaughters, Heather and Ashley, are daughters of Larry and Tony, respectively, both grads in the 1970s. Lynn (think Carma Theatre), graduated from BHS in the early 1950s. Someone told me – can't remember who – that Lynn has two other grandchildren graduating from high school elsewhere. Mitchell Kleman's mother, Kim, and father, Jeff, are both BHS grads. Mitchell's grandmother, Sharon Locke, attended Bluffton schools, as did Sharon's father, Donavan Conrad, who graduated in the early 1920s. Terri Ludwig brought to mind her mother, Bernie, a mid-1970s BHS grad. Bernie's father, Bernard, is generation three. Bernard's mother, Mildred, could be generation four, if only I could confirm it. Then things got complicated. Amber Beasley's mother did not attend BHS, but her grandfather, Marl Watkins did, as did Marl's father, Bob Watkins. Mixed in the pack was a group of extended cousins, which I will no doubt stumble on connecting relationships. But I'll try. Tyler Benjamin's mother, Tina Falk, is a BHS grad. Her mother, Carol, attended BHS. Carol's mother, Treva Lewis did also. Now, listen carefully. Jerilyn Schmutz's parents are BHS grads. Ron is from the class of 1975 and Canda is 1973. Canda's father, Kenny, is a BHS grad. Ron's parents John is a 1951 grad and Sue is a 1954 grad. Sue and her sister, Carol's (see Tyler Benjamin) mother is Treva Lewis. Treva married Dana Mathewson of Ada. Dana's twin brother, Nick, is the father of Gordon, a BHS grad of 1958. Gordon's son, Nick, is a BHS grad, as is his wife, Brenda. Nick and Brenda's daughter, Alyssia, is a '04 grad. Got that? Alyssia's grandmother (on her mother's side), Jane Benroth is also a '59 BHS grad.

Danielle Weyer can match everyone mentioned so far. Sort of. Her father, Kevin, is a 1974 BHS graduate. Danielle's aunt, Annette, attended BHS as did Annette's mother, Mary Lewis, who graduated in 1953. Mary's father, Art, graduated in the

1930s. I tried to figure out several generations back of Travis Swank, Keri Steiner, Penny Suter and Paul Garlock. I knew if I had another week of pondering, I could do it. But my time was up. By the time Danielle sat down, near the end of the alphabet my genealogical mind had overloaded. None of my connections involved the Bluffton-Pandora, Bluffton-Beaverdam, or Bluffton-Mt. Cory relationships, of which there are countless numbers. But, it was time for some speeches. The Bluffton High School class of 2004 is now graduated. As you can see, it weaves its own interesting family relationships to another layer of Bluffton history.

Bluffton vehicle physician diagnoses his last engine noise

Column on the retirement of Jim Kinn – If only auto service centers gave honorary doctorate degrees. Jim Kinn's wall would be covered with them. Try blindfolding him. Then, drive your car through the Stratton Auto Group's Bluffton Auto Repair Center lot. By the vibration of your car's tires he can determine how many miles are left on the treads. His next pronouncement might be a prediction of the life expectancy of your brake drums. On several occasions, we've witnessed him nail these and other obscure vehicle facts and figures within 2,000 miles of the actually number. And, to think, he'd rattle off these equipment projections after he named the car VIN number and whether its transmission fluid needs flushing. Blindfolded! Kinn's final day in his office – with one of the most scenic windows in Bluffton – at the corner of Main and Jefferson was on Dec. 27. As manager of the former Kirtland's Auto Repair and now Bluffton Auto Repair Center, Kinn has had his hands on more cars than might come off the line in Detroit during an entire model year. He's diagnosed Bluffton vehicles' issues since the mid-1980s. His under-the-hood knowledge ranges from engine diagnostics to warranty issues and license plate screws.

Every vehicle he ever sold or worked on has its own story.

Here are two from my own personal vehicle experiences with Kinn: He told me that the Honda I bought used from Kirtland's was originally Mark Yoder's son's car. Mark's son didn't want to sell it because it was the car he drove on his first-ever date, or something like that. When my 2000 Dodge Caravan failed to start, he treated the announcement like a doctor coming out of surgery. "Fred, I've got bad news for you. It's time to call it quits on this car." If you can picture that scene with Kinn shaking his head as if he lost a patient, then you'll understand his connection to his customers and his love for his profession. We are certain most viewers reading this have similar stories to share.

I beat Ben Rothlisberger in a game of horse

Column on a ride around town with Ben Luginbuhl – Ben Luginbuhl, always man-about-town in Bluffton, now of Portland, Oregon, gets at the wheel of his parent's 1994 Dodge Caravan with 198,500 miles logged on it. There was a half tank of gas, peanuts on the floor mat and two cups of Common Grounds coffee to go in the cup holders. He's in town for a few days over Christmas and wants to get caught up on the slander and libel of the place. I want to cruise in my Dodge Caravan. It's an even trade, but the '94 Dodge had more character. He asks me if I've ever bagged it. I say, "No. What is it?" He says you go dumpster diving at McDonald's. Get a tossed out bag, fill it with sand. Duct tape the bag to the roof of your vehicle. Then cruise around town. People start pointing, saying, "Hey, you left your meal on your roof." We didn't do this, but it sounded like a good thing to try. Next thing you know, Ben's talking about everyone on his Lima News paper route. I ask what year we're talking about. He says 1991 when he was a third grader. He and Alison, his sister, had the Harmon, Poplar, East Kibler Street route for several years. Passed it on to Newt Sommer. Later took the Lawn and Grove route, which was larger. About 55 customers at its peak. Made $50 a month. Not bad for a grade school kid in the 1990s. "It was huge cash," he said. "But, you had to leave sleepovers early to collect." Then he started harping about some of the customers on the route. It was pretty interesting. You'll need to inquire about this with him.

This Dec. 26 Bluffton cruise, by the way, included just about every alley in town. Some were forgotten and that made it all the better. We starting talking about people, just as we passed Karim Awad's mother's house on Lawn. There's a sign in Karim's bedroom window – he is visiting from Connecticut – which read "History Matters." We debated the meaning of the sign for one block and then things really got interesting. Several years ago Karim passed around the most fascinating recording of a so-called series of phone calls supposedly taken from his telephone answering machine. Anyone who has heard this knows that the key word is "Dugen," Canadian jive. Seems Karim worked at a cable company. Some guy called in about 20 times in one hour leaving message after message, complaining that his cable was off. Ben and I figured the whole thing was a hoax. It was really too well done. Ben claims Josh Weaver has a copy. He's going to ask Josh to send it to me. Just then we turned from Kibler on to Main and saw Jon Wietholder turn from Main to Kibler. Must be headed for Sunset. Seeing Jon reminded Ben that he was once on a Bluffton Little League baseball team with Ben Roethlisberger. Jon's dad, Brad, was the coach. "I beat Ben (Roethlisberger) in horse," says Ben-at-the-wheel. I marveled at this fact as we headed north on Main. Meanwhile other names that entered the conversation included Mike Mooney, Roger Brodman, who we saw walking down the street, Julia Hangsen, who lives in Ashville, North Carolina, and some guy, who was on Ben's Lima News paper route. I asked Ben if Newt Sommer was still collecting Soviet Union memorabilia. Ben didn't know anything about that phase of Newt's life, so I went on to someone else. By then the CNB time and temp read 12:12. I exited the Caravan. Took a pix of Ben. Said, "See you later," and off he cruised into the haze of Bluffton. Just then I realized I left my coffee in the coffee holder. Even so, it was the most interesting 61 minutes I'd spent in some time.

Pruning time
FROM JOHN MOSER, VIA DICK BOEHR

You could always tell when spring was in the air by my father's announcement that "it's pruning time." So, we would get all the pruning equipment ready – the saws, shears, loppers and whatever – to sharpen them. It made the pruning job a lot easier. It's one thing to cut a one-inch branch at hip height. It's another thing to cut the same size branch extending as far as you can reach, contorted around some blocking branches all the while standing on one leg on a ladder. Then we would go to the orchard and decide which trees to remove. The reasons for pruning are three-fold: it makes for larger, better, healthier fruit; it protects the tree from too much fruit that could break the branches during a wind storm; and the owner can control the size and shape of the tree. With that in mind, we cut off all dead, diseased and broken limbs. We prune water sprouts rather heavily, but we save some. Choices are much easier to make following the screening process. Cherry trees don't need much pruning. Pear, apple, plum and especially peach take much more. How much more was an open question.

The following illustration describes the decision-making process: First, prune the peach tree as much as you think necessary. Second, go over it again and take about half of the remaining branches. Third, locate yourself about 12 feet from the tree. There were usually cats following us in the orchard, looking for mice or just being sociable. Reach down and get a cat by the tail and throw it forceably into the tree. If the cat passes through the tree without catching a branch, the tree was pruned sufficiently. If the cat caught a branch, more pruning was necessary.

Grafting was done at the same time. My father did all that, but I have tried my hand at that just this last week. It included keeping the graft, or scions, in the freezer to keep them dormant. Pruning and grafting along with refining and disciplining are mentioned frequently in the Bible, with much the same purpose: to produce good fruit and to protect the tree or vines so that they don't go to foliage or non-essentials, or in the case of refining, to burn out the impurities. After all, you can't eat foliage. You want just enough foliage to produce good fruit. Fruit is the object. But, frail human that I am, I'd rather be the pruner than the prunee.

Making a point

"Literature is full of wanting to go home again themes. Much local history is written in the nostalgic spirit of this fundamental human impulse to seek the security known in younger days in place and time and society. Even if we can't really go home again – particularly in our overcharged time – the love and faithfulness implicit in that impulse are important elements in recreating the historic spirit that has marked out the destinies of the place."

Gordon E. Alderfer, 1933 Bluffton High School graduate, wrote those words in his essay "Some Reflections on the Writing of Local History." Whether the Bluffton of his own past swirled in his thoughts when writing this, we don't know. Referring to Alderfer, Robert Kreider adds an interesting recollection of him in Kreider's introduction to this book on page 10. As a junior and senior, Alderfer was a member of the Bluffton High School debate team, coached by Paul Stauffer, that won two consecutive Ohio Scholastic debate championships. Reflecting upon going home again jump out in the following brief statements from persons who grew up in Bluffton, several of whom no longer live here. These glimpses come from interviews posted on the Bluffton Icon plus other conversations we've enjoyed over the last decade.

Lauren Canaday

On Aug. 17, 2017, the Bluffton Public Library held a "Great American Solar Eclipse" watch party. We passed out special sunglasses for people to watch the eclipse. Dozens of patrons participated in this once-in-a-lifetime event on the library lawn. One library patron, who missed it, came in the library and asked if we planned to reschedule it. Can you believe that?

Dave Bracy

During the 1974 derby, I was fishing with my family in our usual spot, right across from the shelter house. Halfway through the derby I suddenly got a hit on my daredevil lure. I reeled the fish in to see that it was a trout. As my dad helped me net the trout and get it on the bank, we noticed it had a tag on its mouth. I asked dad what number it was and I thought he was going to have a heart attack right then and there. It was tag number one! Dad was really nervous as we walked over to the shelter house to turn it in. From then on I had my high school nickname of "Big Arb," after the number one fish named for Arden Baker.

Diana Hilty Marshall

The old grade school had a bell tower and I remember the wooden floors and coat closets. We also had the old style bolted-to-the-floor wooden desks with ink wells. One day my pigtails were dipped in the ink well in the desk behind. The culprit will not be named here but he may remember the event.

Jamil Bazzy

High school teacher Mr. Brown was especially entertaining

128

and engaging with his experiments. Once he was cutting chunks of some material (magnesium?) that had to be kept wet or it would burst into flames. A piece popped off and landed in the pocket of his shirt, and his shirt burst into flames. He also had us make nitrogen trioxide, an explosive so sensitive a fly landing on it could set it off. His class could never be called boring. On another subject, there's a tradition of getting a melon helmet your first year working at Suter's Produce. It's the one where you get the most rotten, bug-infested melon slammed on your head when you weren't expecting it. Mine was pretty clean because I had an older brother who worked there also. Others got melons that could gag a maggot.

Amanda Rhonemus

I can honestly say that I loved being in marching band in high school. There was actually an award created for me called the "I Love Marching Band More Than Life Itself" award. It was one of those things that people made fun of, but I absolutely loved. I don't know that I can put the feeling into words, but I can say that I always have and always will be a marching band geek.

Scott Hey

Most school pranks were "paddled" out of my generation during the middle school years at Beaverdam in the mid-1970s. Most fifth and sixth grade teachers back then had a practice of reserving an upper corner section of their chalk boards to record the trouble makers names along with the number of warnings called "marks." Three "marks" would get you three "whacks" and I recall them being quite stout swings. On one occasion Charles Weisenbarger took the fall for several of us and was held up after gym class to receive (our) punishment.

Being the team player, I offered him my pair of skateboard knee pads, which he cleverly concealed in the seat of his pants. The shop teacher, "Mr. Z" eagerly volunteered to give his "lesson" to "Barger." Mr. Z had one of the most intimidating wooden paddles of them all. We were told it was illegal for the paddles to have holes drilled all the way through, but his was creatively drilled only half way, which could leave an interesting pattern on your rear (but not this time).

From our vantage point it sounded like years of pent up frustration was being channeled into each blow as they echoed out into the hallway. I don't know if Mr. Z ever found out that we tricked him, but when "Barger" came back out in the hallway he was smiling as he handed me back the padding leaving Mr. Z likely baffled and thinking to himself, "that son of a dentist sure has a tough butt."

Tim Neufeld
Before coming to Bluffton my family lived in Belgian Congo. I attended first, second and third grades there. I spoke English and a little Lingala dialect. This is a strange story, but when our family lived in the Congo, Mobutu, then dictator, ran over our dog when I was a kid. There was a motorcade with motorcycles and Mobutu's limo. The limo hit the dog. He never stopped. I think Mobutu was eventually overthrown.

Jessica Edmiston
Once in the fifth grade I got my card taken down for hitting Nick Houshower in the face with the playground tetherball when he wasn't playing by the rules. I had to stay after school and write a paper about how hitting him made me feel and what I had learned. Sorry, Nick.

Joe Goodman
One day Rick Ramseyer discovered his dad's hidden cache of fireworks. Inside were a couple of "silver salutes" – about twice the power of an M-80 firecracker. So, we thought it would be awesome to test one out at their home near the golf course. We

blew an 8-inch chunk of asphalt cleanly out of the road and our ears rang for most of the day. I don't think Dick and Elfrieda were very impressed, but we were believers.

Richard Minck

Theola Steiner was my favorite teacher. She taught sixth grade. All the boys thought she was all right. After school one day, I had to get something. I saw her up ahead. I'm at the stairway. A middle-aged guy came up and she hugged him. That ruined it.

And, please tell us about the Bluffton rumor that you made a piece of jewelry for Marlon Brando. (Shocked expression from Richard.) I don't remember. That was one of my first trips to California. I had a shop, thought people would be pouring in. No one showed up. I was introduced to the Hollywood group in the late 1950s. I went to a party, met a Hollywood starlet, she asked what I did, connected me, and I did a piece for someone. I don't know if it was Brando.

Alee Gratz-Collier

You want to know what it's like being the daughter of the town postmaster? Kind of annoying. I'm not going to lie. People automatically know me. They say that I act and look like him. When I tell people that I'm the postmaster's daughter they say, "Oh, yeah." I can never get away with anything because he's going to find out.

Courtney Goode

I took my driver's test in a white, 1986 Dodge Aries station wagon lovingly known as "the grocery-getter." I did indeed pass the test the first time. Despite starting out with one strike against me – the car was ghastly – and suffering strike two during the test itself when I crossed a railroad track without stopping or slowing down, I was able to successfully parallel park her and avoided strike three. A week later, I got my first speeding ticket.

Micah Sommer

My grandfather, Dick Weaver, homeschooled my siblings, a handful of cousins, and me. With him I spent most of my time building bird feeders and puppet theaters, visiting museums, writing short stories, and going on treasure hunts. I entered Bluffton schools in fourth grade but my first public school experience was the year before, when my mom took a sabbatical to teach in Nicaragua and hauled the whole family along. My Spanish vocabulary as I began at school consisted of the words for "Hello" and "I need to use the bathroom." I used both phrases my first day.

Ben Kruse

I received one "Saturday school." It was for something two friends did, some minor graffiti. Anyway a group of about six of us were indicted for the crime. Our punishment was to spend Saturday cleaning the graffiti under the semi-supervision of the janitor, Delmer Nuzum. I brought in doughnuts for everyone, we played basketball in the gym, raced on those old square boards with wheels, and in the final 20 minutes we threw some soapy water on the graffiti and called it a day.

James Pannabecker

In Kindergarten, some of us went to Crow's because they were giving away free balloons. When we returned, Miss Groman asked everyone who went to Crow's to stand up. I didn't stand, but went to Crow's. Everyone who stood up received a spanking. I didn't get spanked and felt bad about it for the next five years. I probably never lied in the next five years either.

In second grade, with Mrs. Klay, we once played out in the snow. When we came in she had us all take off our pants and hang them in the cloak room to dry. We wore our coats while our pants dried.

Sam Diller

Dave Risser who ran the coffee shop where 10,000 Villages is located was in charge of the food during the Bluffton rodeo one year. He bought hot dogs from a business in Findlay. Sometime after the rodeo the person who supplied the hot dogs was indicted and later pled guilty to a charge of putting horsemeat in the 'dogs. My dad's insurance office was above Risser's coffee shop. Dad said the morning Risser read the horsemeat story in The Courier he turned the air blue with bad words, which could be heard up and down Main Street.

Jeremy Szabo

Back in the early 1970s several Bluffton youth were skinny dipping in the National Quarry, now known as Cob Lake. Patrolman Wade Bechtel found the kids' clothes and took them. This happened in the middle of the night. One wonders how the kids got home.

In the early 1970s the Szabo family had a dog named Nipper. He was a Welsh terrier mutt and he would just nip at you and never bite. Our neighbor, Arden Baker, would put out pans of beer to kill the slugs in his garden. One summer day we began to notice Nipper sleeping a lot during the day and Arden's beer pans were empty but the garden still had slugs. The dog had been consuming the beer. Needless to say this really amused Arden and the entire neighborhood. We had a dog with a drinking problem.

Jaye Bumbaugh

Elmer Neufeld once asked me, "Jaye, what is art?" I told him, "Elmer, your signature is art." (Elmer's signature was unique and difficult to read.)

Living where we live

Do you have any idea how exotic this place

Bluffton University Nature Preserve, Ohio: Winter Liminal

BY DAVE ESSINGER

The snow in the fields is crisscrossed by finger-wide tracks, and otherwise pristine. One might imagine sticks dragged by wandering wraiths, absent-minded visitors from the other side, but with no other marks at all, at first I can't guess what really made these traces.

Eventually it dawns on me that the tracks are made from beneath the surface and not above: mice moving under the snow. It's another "other side," a real other realm, and a reminder: not everything we register at the interface of our world originates there.

The mouse-trails wind and cross and begin and disappear, and show up in any depth of snow, but they never break the surface that I can see. I imagine furry mouse-submariners pawing and digging, navigating by scent and temperature and pressure and dead reckoning, never breaching periscope depth. I wonder if lazier mice re-use others' tunnels or, lacking that kind of foresight, they just go, honeycombing the snow, and with each new errand, extending. We see only the most peripheral capillaries of a vast temporary circulatory network. Mouse-bodies moving like blood, pushed by the beat of a heart bigger than them, bigger than any of us.

My own blood pushes up beneath my exposed skin, a constant heat-exchange, a one-sided streaming toward entropy. It's five degrees below zero, and I'm not dressed for contemplation. My eyelashes bead and freeze from my breath.

From here, I could run out on the ice of the lake, above slumbering fish in the grave-cold muck, their own suspended dimension. The ice could be a bridge to tiny islands I only see from shore in summer. It also might break beneath me – there's no knowing its thickness.

No one knows I'm here.

Suddenly, right at my feet, here is a new trail being made: a raised line, a mouse meandering, a drawing tracing itself. I watch the snow lift as the mouse burrows along. The arched roof of the tunnel lasts for a while, and I imagine the light shining through, blue-white, the snow holding its dome in the wake of the warm mouse bullet body that made it.

Some trails must end in a scuffle: there are foxes, owls. Prowling cats. I could excavate the one in front of me, crash its ceiling, let in annihilating light with my shoe. Untouched, it will end in silent powdery collapse – and then vanish with wind, or melt, or new snow.

I'm in a moving mandala, traces on a membrane that draws and erases itself. Already, I've stood still too long, the cold grasping for me across all these liminal boundary layers.

No one knows I'm here.

Cottage cheese
BY JOANNE NISWANDER

I wish Dean were still alive to tell you this story in person, but you'll have to put up with my telling it. Even then, I have heard this story in bits and pieces. Also, long years after the fact. So you'll have to take it all in with a grain of salt. My late husband, Dean Niswander, was a "townie" growing up on

South Main Street. His family's home was one of those neat two-story turn-of-the-century houses – this one just across the alley from the funeral home. It was the mid-1930s. The time of dads at work, moms at home, and young kids pretty much obeying the rules and trying to keep out of trouble while still having fun. At the time of his story, Dean was probably seven or eight (I'm just guessing). Old enough to be familiar with the neighborhood but not old enough to roam at will. Occasionally, he was allowed to go uptown to the "store" with his father, Carey, who sold the familiar red Farmall tractors (and other stuff) to area farmers. Sometimes he was sent to a neighbor to borrow a little of this or a little of that, as neighbors tended to do in those days. Sometimes his mother took him along when she went down the street to visit her friend, Mrs. Diller, where Dean had the opportunity to play with her son Sherwood's toys (Sherwood's claim to fame was his not-so-permanent marriage to comedienne Phyllis Diller). Anyway, that's how life went on apace in Bluffton.

Now, in case you don't remember where things were in Bluffton back in those days, the Page Dairy was an important business located in the area where the high school soccer field is now. Just a hop-skip-and-jump from the Niswander home. If you lived nearby, you could just walk down to the Page Dairy building with your container and buy fresh milk and other dairy products there. The farm at your doorstep. One sunny afternoon Dean's mother had an errand for him to run. It was his job to walk down Main Street to Poplar, then turn left and go to the Page Dairy to get some fresh cottage cheese for supper. A good job for a kid with nothing else to do. She handed him a small lidded pail and a quarter. The pail was for cottage cheese, dipped right out of the vat. The quarter was for payment. Now, I must tell you a little about the pail that Dean carried. It was small – a good fit for young hands. There were two handles at either side of the pail, plus two small clamps, to assure that the lid was held secure. There was also an additional handle at the top of the lid for easy carrying when the pail was light-weight and empty. "Be sure to carry the pail in both hands on the way home," his mother had warned. He'd heard that before. I think you know where this story is going. So, let's get on with it. The trip to the Page Dairy was uneventful. Everything as usual. But it was such a beautiful day. Dean got his cottage cheese, paid for it, and was whistling his way home up Poplar Street to Main – when the inevitable happened. Yes, he had forgotten his mother's warning and was carrying the bucket of cottage cheese by the lid, swinging it as he had on the way to the dairy. Suddenly down went the bucket – upside down, of course. Cottage cheese was everywhere. What to do?

Well, Dean did what any good Boy Scout would do. With his hands, and with help from the lid, he scooped up as much of the cottage cheese as he could and put it back in the container. Probably wiped his hands on his pants before walking the rest of the way home. At home, Dean's mom lifted the lid and said, "Why, there's not as much cottage cheese in here as we usually get." Dean's answer was most serious. "They didn't have very much left so that's all they gave us this time." And that was that – until suppertime when Dad got home from work. The two men had a private "discussion" that included two lessons – one on the subject of gravitational pull and the other on the subject of truth. There may have been a harder lesson as well, but Dean never mentioned too much about that. Anyway, the lessons made their point. It wasn't until later that Dean discovered that it was a neighbor on Poplar Street (a good friend of his mother) who snitched on him. She saw the bucket drop and chuckled over the scrambled recovery of cottage cheese. She then quickly went to the phone to let Dean's mother know that the cottage cheese delivery would be a bit delayed (and a bit scant). Of course, they didn't have cottage cheese for supper that evening. Dean may not have been sitting during supper, either. If he had supper at all.

My brother Norman
BY JOANNE NISWANDER

Everybody in town likes him. At least, that's the way it appears. Come to think of it, I guess I like him too – now. Now that he's grown up. He's really come a long way. My brother used to be a pain. It's no fun having a brother when you're a little kid, living on a farm, with no other girls living close enough to play with. Especially when your brother's years and years older than you – four and a half years older, to be exact. Naturally, he wasn't interested in playing with his little sister. Lucky for him, a boy his age lived on the farm just down the road. So, you can see that he had someone else to play with. Do you think they'd let me play with them? No way. They didn't want any girls. And, when it was just Norman and me at home, life was miserable then, too. See, he liked to tease me and play tricks on me. I guess there's just something born into big brothers that makes them that way. Besides that, since he was a lot older than I was, he could get the best of me every time – and get away with it. I don't know how he did it. Being oldest, Norman always got what he wanted first – before I could even think about what I wanted. Let me give you a good example: He got a chemistry set for Christmas one year. And that chemistry set grew, and grew, and grew until he finally had his own separate room in the house for his chemistry lab. People would "ooh" and "aah" over it just like it was something really special. I thought it smelled.

Then there was the marimba. That's what he played all during high school. Probably even before high school, but I don't remember for sure. What I do remember is that it took up a lot of room in the house. Norm was good at it, I guess. At least that's what people said. Mom would haul him all over the countryside to contests and programs. Of course, I had to go along, too. I was too little to stay home by myself. So I had to help take the marimba apart and carry it to the car (you had to take it apart and put it back together, you know). When we got to where we were going, we had to lug the pieces into the building where he was going to play. Then, after the program, we did it all over again. Some fun that was. Nobody knew who I was, except that I was Norm Vercler's little sister. Sometimes I had the privilege of turning pages for him while he played something on the marimba. Big Deal! The only time that was fun was in the summer. You see, in the summer we had band concerts in town every week and Norman accompanied the soloists on his marimba, since there wasn't a piano in the band shell. The high school girls who sang had to come to our house to practice. Since I was the page turner, I got to sit right there with the "big girls" and admire their clothes and hairdos and listen to them laugh about school stuff. But they didn't really pay any attention to me. I was just part of the furniture. And the other obnoxious thing about Norm was that he was always telling jokes. Always. And people laughed, too. I didn't laugh.

Finally, Norm graduated from high school and went away to college. I didn't miss him – very much. At last I had a chance to be someone other than Norm Vercler's little sister. And, in the meantime, Norm was getting a little nicer and a little more considerate and – well, just nicer. College must have started to mellow him. Well, I finally graduated from high school and came to Bluffton to go to college. Norman stayed in Illinois. But later, after we both were married and had started to raise our families, Norm moved his family to Bluffton and they bought a house right across Main Street from ours. You know, Norm and Mary Lou and their girls just seemed to fit right in to Bluffton life. Norm worked at Bluffton Hospital – the first X-ray technician they ever had. And, in his spare time, he fixed everybody's radio in his basement workshop at home. Then he started solving their TV problems. And after retiring from his hospital work, he opened his own radio-TV repair shop. Right smack in the middle of downtown Bluffton. He ended up being a very popular downtown businessman, no less. You know, it's amazing how Norm had REALLY CHANGED. He was still a tease and people still laughed at his jokes. But his jokes were a lot funnier than they used to be back in Illinois. I even laughed every once in a while. Like I said, people in town seem to like him. He's always ready with a smile and a helping hand. Even for his little sister, who finally grew up enough to appreciate what she had all along.

Bluffton? What's that?

BY JOANNE NISWANDER

What is Bluffton? What words best depict this place where we live? Or, conversely, what words describe what this place is not? Where do we start? Let's start out by saying that Bluffton is a village - or is it a town? My Webster's unabridged tells me that a village is "a group of houses in the country, smaller than a town or city and larger than a hamlet." Webster goes on to define the word "town" as "a more or less concentrated group of houses and private and public buildings, larger than a village but smaller than a city." Well, Bluffton does have houses, plus private and public buildings, so let's say we're a town. Where is Bluffton? Is it in northwest Ohio or west central Ohio? It's definitely in the western part of Ohio, but Bluffton is not quite so obviously located in the north-south category. It's sort of on the south edge of the north part of western Ohio and the north edge of the central part. Oh, but there's one important reference point. Bluffton lies along Interstate 75, midway between Lima and Findlay. Or, to the more geographically challenged, halfway between Toledo and Dayton. Yes, we're on the map. What kind of community is this Bluffton of ours? Bluffton must be a "rural" community because there are farms surrounding it. If so, then what differentiates Bluffton from Columbus Grove or Fort Jennings or Spencerville? Bluffton

140

must be a "college" community because a college is located here. So what differentiates it from Ada or Wilmington or Defiance? Bluffton must be an "industrial" community because there are various industries here. Then what differentiates it from Ottawa or North Baltimore or Kenton? Bluffton must be a "retirement" community because it has a nursing home and assisted living facilities – plus many retirees live here. Then what differentiates it from Arlington or Delphos or Leipsic? Who lives in Bluffton? Young folks and old folks and those in between. People who were born here and those who just moved in. Uncles and grandmas and some who aren't related to anyone. Retired farmers and young college professors. Involved citizens and those who don't give a hoot. Veterans and pacifists. Bird watchers and deer hunters. Church-goers and Sunday sleepers-in. An assortment of people much like in any other not-very-big Ohio community. So what makes us different? What goes on in Bluffton? What doesn't go on in Bluffton, one might ask instead. If you hanker for an athletic event to attend, most likely there will be at least one going on (if not half a dozen) every night of the week, including all summer. If music is your wish, you can find the classics at Bluffton University recitals, home-grown talent at public school programs, anything from bluegrass to jazz at the town hall concerts as well as the coffeehouse and the library. There are multiple special goings-on throughout the year, including the annual fishing derby, arts and crafts festival, and the big Christmas-season Blaze of Lights. In addition, there's the summer-long Saturday farmer's market (plus numerous chicken barbecues) to keep your family well fed, enough churches to keep your family well blessed, and enough doctors in the area to keep your family healthy, plus a hospital in case of emergency. So, what is Bluffton not? Bluffton's not big. It's not perfect. But it's home.

My life in Bluffton as a Scout, 1956-1965
BY DAVID REMPEL SMUCKER

The Cub Scouts had "Den Mothers," leaders for each group, and my mother Irene took her turn. For example, in April 1958, our den took a hike on the Bluffton College campus to identify flowers and trees. My mother typed an account in which she listed 14 different flowers and 14 different trees, which she identified for the boys. A short mimeographed Cub Scout newsletter from January 1959 shows that Garth Gerber, David Smucker, John Lehman, Gregg Luginbuhl, and John Simcox were in this den. My journalism beat as a 9-year-old was "Local News" in our "newspaper." I reported on a mild physical attack suffered by this group of boys, perpetrated by a group of three older boys, whom I named in the article: "The lesson is: do not pick on kids littler than you." I am surprised at the boldness of my journalistic muckraking. The Boy Scouts had been in Bluffton since 1939. Our congregation, First Mennonite Church, served as the sponsor of Troop 256 from 1939 to 1988. Boys and leaders from different church denominations participated in the scouting program. In Boy Scouts we learned outdoor skills – set up camp, make fires, tie knots, identify trees and plants (poison ivy! and poison sumac!), handle canoes, deal with snake bites, purify water, cook on fires, operate rowboats and canoes, do simple first aid. Other skills included leading orderly meetings and developing group social skills outside school and church settings. We would usually spend one week per year at Camp Berry near Findlay. We occasionally did overnight hikes in southern Ohio, where the hills contrasted with the flatland of Allen County. The Boy Scout Oath, which we memorized and recited: "On my honor I will do my best, to do my duty to God and my country, and to obey the Scout Law, to help other people at all times, to keep myself physically strong, mentally awake, and morally straight." We also memorized and recited the Scout Law, which are 12

142

personality characteristics: trustworthy, loyal, helpful, friendly, courteous, kind, obedient, cheerful, thrifty, brave, clean and reverent. Many important dynamics for character formation are compressed in this Oath and Law. As world-renown biologist and Eagle Scout, E. O. Wilson, reflects on the oath, "You try to say it better in that many words." I have not perfectly kept to all points of that Scout Oath and Law, but it has stood as a meaningful goal for my entire life.

Scoutmasters during the early 1960s were Don Badertscher and then Warren Eastman (with his two boys, Cliff and Max). Warren, a Methodist, was a gregarious and hands-on Scout leader, who participated himself in most of the hikes and camping experiences. My father Carl had some terms as Institutional Representative, a kind of link, I suspect, between the congregation and the Scouting administrative structure. My good friend Gregg Luginbuhl and I were in Boy Scouts together, but not another good friend, Garth Gerber, son of the local photographers, Leland and Winifred Gerber. If I remember correctly, his parents disallowed that, due to their religious convictions; perhaps they objected to the uniforms, reminiscent of the armed forces and the "oath" terminology. In order to obtain the status of Eagle Scout one had to earn at least 21 merit badges. I received these merit badges between June 22, 1963, and June 15, 1964: rowing, music, hiking, public speaking, firemanship, Indian lore, scholarship, canoeing, animal husbandry, pioneering, camping, cooking, citizenship in the community, citizenship in the nation, nature, soil and water conservation, personal fitness, first aid, swimming, lifesaving, and safety. I also have the merit badge books on insect life and journalism, but I apparently did not earn those. One scouting highlight for me was the Nature Merit Badge. I would meet with Herbert Berky, science professor at the college, on Saturdays and receive instruction on identification of plants and birds and trees and animals.

He took an interest in me. Since both of my grandfathers had died before my birth, I think that he served as a partial surrogate grandfather. My current interest in these subjects must have been augmented by H. W., in addition to my own father's interest in birding. [Later in the 1970s as a young adult I visited him in Bluffton, when he reflected on changes in his profession. He remarked that as a young scientist he and his colleagues had very little sense of what we know as the environmental crisis brought about by excessive industrialization. They were not yet aware of the scope of impact that human-induced pollution could inflict on the environment. He expressed some slight regret that he had not earlier realized these insights.]

Working with our First Mennonite pastor Jacob Friesen, I attained the God and Country merit badge on Feb. 9, 1963. This was a crucial juncture in my understanding of an appropriate sense of being a grateful citizen of the United States without compromising my Christian convictions, especially those regarding biblical pacifism. After garnering the top Boy Scout status of the Eagle Scout Award in 1964, along with Bruce Marshall and John Pannabecker, I joined what is called the Order of the Arrow, an "elite" group of the Boy Scouts. Older guys in this group included Lee Cookson and Tom Brauen, who I think continued in the organization as leaders. This involved being chosen by other Order of the Arrow scouts. It was dramatically done at an evening campfire and subsequent experience, called the Ordeal, at Camp Berry near Findlay. The candidates filed past the chief near the fire. The chosen one felt a hand come down on his shoulder, being "tapped," then he was immediately taken away, blindfolded, and deposited in the woods. The test was to survive the entire night in the woods without any tent or materials, or food. I remember a fitful sleep on the hard ground with some leaves for padding, the growling of my stomach, and the joy at seeing the sunrise – until I was able in the morning to wander into an area with people. During the next day, candidates maintained silence, received small amounts of food, and worked on camp improvement projects. Subsequently, I bought materials from kits to make various Indian objects, such as a head-dress, loincloth, vest, all which had beaded pieces sewed on. I worked avidly with a small loom doing beading for my Order of the Arrow costumes. My mother's considerable skill in sewing certainly made this possible, although I did a lot of the work myself. After donning our costumes, we memorized and practiced group Indian dancing movements and performed them at scouting functions. In my second or third year of high school I left both the Boy Scouts and the Order of the Arrow.

Reflections on my Bluffton High School years, 1963-1967
BY DAVID REMPEL SMUCKER

In high school I concentrated on course work, basketball, and a few extra-curricular activities. Harriet (Criblez) Luginbuhl taught Latin and I had two or three years learning a "dead" language that became very useful in many future contexts. Latin helped expand my English vocabulary, prepared me for French in college, helped me understand Roman Catholic worship, and provided a vocabulary advantage for my future trips to continental Europe. For an astounding 47 years (1935-1982) Florence Duffield (1913-2011) taught students to type, a skill that she enabled me to use – at this very minute. (Thanks, Miss Duffield, and also for the $1.6 million you willed to the Bluffton Public Library.) With little interest or aptitude in mathematics, I enrolled in Bruce Moyer's small calculus class. Mr. Moyer was such an excellent teacher that he motivated me to truly enjoy, for a brief time, studying math, a pleasure I have subsequently never again experienced. On the other side of the column was a teacher from West Virginia, who enjoyed talking about himself – his exploits military and his opinions – more than teaching.

Thankfully, he only did a year or two of damage in Bluffton.

Acting in dramas in high school really engaged me, which probably reflected my paternal grandfather's love of the dramatic stage. The emotional Mr. Persinger directed dramas. In my junior year I had one of the main roles in "Charley's Aunt," an impersonation in a dress of the aunt of my friend Charley, played by Bob Hilty. Other organizations were: National Honor Society, Latin Club president (sophomore), Mixed Chorus, Boys Glee Club, and Student Senate (freshman). James Hahn as choir and glee club conductor always urged us to a higher level of singing, even though he was not able to achieve the disciplined concentration that he desired. As I peruse those ancient high school yearbooks, I note that some other students participated in many more extra-curricular activities than I chose. I probably studied more than some other students.

One memorable teenage experience pertained to a July 4 night, when a group of us were celebrating in a car. We had been out in the country setting off firecrackers and decided to drive through Bluffton to the country on the other side of town. Some foreign guest of one of us did not realize the accepted conventions, and tossed out some lighted firecrackers right on Main Street. The policeman (Carter Shisler or Kaiser Gaiffe) in their nearby cruiser quickly caught us and took us to the police station. He gave us a very stern lecture and said that he was going to contact our parents about this event. Shaken and penitent, we quickly decided as a group that we would go to each of the parents and explain the embarrassing situation. My disappointed parents said that we should have known better, as did the others, except one set of parents was much more disappointed. That was uncomfortable to undergo. Since no charges were filed, I don't think we suffered any permanent legal damage. The sheriff never did telephone our parents (unless they never told us).

From my earliest years I had enjoyed playing basketball. Dad put a basket and board out back, and I spent many hours practicing. In the evening there was a special feeling of jumping up to shoot the ball and being finally unable to see the hoop. Sometimes I continued to play long after the sun set, and it was too dark to see. Basketball was serious business for me, even, in the eighth grade, deciding for it rather than piano lessons with James Bixel. A wrong turn in life? (How ironic that today I play piano almost every day and never play basketball.) In this endeavor I was knit closely to Gregg Luginbuhl and Jim Ehrman. Usually at the guard position, my 6 feet height provided an advantage over the usually shorter guards.

The high point of my quite average career was certainly my junior or senior year in the Holiday Tournament, a tiny Christmas season tournament at the college Founders Hall between Bluffton, Cory-Rawson, Pandora-Gilboa and Buckeye Local. For the first game with Cory-Rawson, I scored 21 points, 9 baskets and 3 foul shots. We won 53 to 50. For the second title game with Buckeye Local, we won 52 to 48 in overtime. With only 6 seconds left in the game, we were 2 points behind. I was fouled and calmly sank 2 foul shots, sending the game into overtime. (Tragically, I forget who scored the winning overtime points!) It was my only (and fleeting) experience of being a sports hero and probably helped me to win the Most Valuable Player (MVP) trophy for 1967. Year-end statistics for my senior year (1966-67) show Jim Ehrman leading with 312 total points, then Gregg Luginbuhl with 207, then Nelson White with 168, then yours truly with 149. In earlier years as a young boy I had imagined many more victories in our high school years than we in fact gained. Feeling the sting of disappointment, I knew for the first time that our imagined basketball glories had passed us by, and we would never again have a chance to "right that wrong." No basketball in my college future. Our basketball team was constantly being compared to the football team, which in 1966 had a 9-0 record and had many talented players, especially Jim Opperman. Characteristic is the following quote from a newspaper account: "Last fall Bluffton had one of the best football teams in the state. And one of their trademarks was never let the opposition get close. Not much rubbed off on the basketball team apparently." Although not overtly, it seemed to some of us that Coach Mark Covert concentrated his attention on football rather than basketball. I thought he was a competent basketball coach in terms of strategy. Even though I earned an athletic "letter" B (and still have it), I never bought a Pirates jacket, on which to display the letter, or joined the athletic organization, Varsity B. Looking back, perhaps that "boycott" immaturely showed my resentment to the attention lavished on the football team.

Another one of my athletic classmate friends was Jim Opperman. Jim exuded what is called "presence." He was very big (6 feet, 4 inches, 235 pounds), very strong, very emotional, and had a "short fuse," that is, a temper. He excelled in athletics, as a football lineman and as a track shot putter and discus-thrower he was rated among the best in the entire state of Ohio. I played with him on the basketball team, a game that did not quite fit his temper and bulk. Jim's father was the local German Reformed pastor, Vernon Opperman, who tragically and painfully died in 1958 of cancer, when Jim was 9. On the day of our graduation in 1967 after the ceremony, Jim buttonholed fellow classmates, including me, and appealed to us: "Don't you realize? This is it. We may never see each other again." A voice of honesty crying in the wilderness. Sadly, I don't remember any response by me to these meaningful questions by someone who knew the impact of endings.

Carved in stone on the exterior of the high school one reads: "The fountain of wisdom flows through books." The school and town tried to emphasize that idea when they placed the town library and the high school library together in the high school building. For many decades, including my time of 1963-1967, Miss Ocie Anderson led that library.

Students were encouraged to use the library and borrow books and magazines. Fortunately, the town later, in 1986, built its own building on Main Street – an excellent and more highly developed library than the one in my memories of high school.

Getting acquainted with Bluffton in the Fifties
BY RUTH NAYLOR

In the autumn of 1952, my brother and I headed across the state into what was for us completely new territory. We were looking for the little town of Bluffton. We had both graduated from Olney Friends Boarding School located in the beautiful hills of southeastern Ohio about 30 miles from where we had grown up. We had never before seen the contrasting flat lands of northwestern Ohio. We'd heard of Mennonites and the Amish, of course, but didn't know any personally. We'd both loved life at the boarding school, which was established near Barnesville, Ohio, and widely supported by conservative Quakers. My maternal grandparents still wore the "plain" Quaker garb and could easily have been mistaken for Amish. Although the dress code at Olney did not require black bonnets or white prayer coverings, there were more restrictions than I cared to continue – such as not being permitted to wear red clothing or any jewelry other than a wrist watch. My limited knowledge of Mennonites had led me to carefully study photos of students in Bluffton College's introductory materials before applying for admission. I wanted to move beyond being told what I could or could not wear, but there were other things in the written Code of Campus Conduct that reflected my Quaker upbringing and that I appreciated: no drinking, smoking or dancing. Popular magazines in the early 1950s encouraged young women to "dress to impress" when making their debut on a college campus. That included, among other things, a hat and gloves. I wanted to get started on the right foot in Bluffton. I'd even seen a photo of the then president of the Student Christian Association and decided that he was one I definitely wanted to meet and impress. It was a lazy afternoon in town when we arrived and things were even quieter on campus. There were no welcome signs or directions, but we stopped in front of College Hall. The drive went completely around the building in those days. We were obviously among the first students to arrive and were wondering where we needed to check in. There wasn't a soul in sight. For several minutes, we sat there discussing what to do next when my brother looked in the rear-view mirror and saw someone coming through the woods between Musselman Library and College Hall. The woman was wearing a long black dress and a little black bonnet. She could easily have passed for the grandmother I fully respected but did not want to emulate. Nevertheless, I carefully slipped off my white gloves and reluctantly removed my earrings. Very shortly after the woman passed our car, a casually dressed coed came out the front door of College Hall; she greeted us and offered to show us to our dorms. On the way to Lincoln Hall where I was to live, we met another student who gushingly congratulated my guide and asked to see her new diamond ring. Lively chatter ensued and I discovered that she had just become engaged to the president of the Student Christian Association. This was my introduction to what became two very good years at Bluffton College before my own Mr. Wonderful graduated and took me with him. Incidentally, I never saw that older woman in "plain dress" on campus again. I was told, though, that it would have been Sarah Nusbaum who lived across Bentley Road behind the college library. In doing a bit of fact-checking, I discovered that she used to be Del Gratz's babysitter when he was a child.

A couple of professors and classes I'll never forget
BY RUTH NAYLOR

I recall distractions in sociology class. I'd seen a few squirrels at a distance before, but they were common here in Bluffton, playing freely in the woods surrounding campus buildings, running across the streets and lawns. But sometimes a beautiful grey squirrel would come to sit on the sill of our ground-level sociology classroom window. I was fascinated with my chance to observe nature so closely. Another sort of distraction happened inside that classroom. Some of the freshman girls (including two Bluffton locals that I'll not name) made it a point to discombobulate the middle-aged professor by sitting in the first row. They would cross their legs and seductively pull their skirts above their knees. Back in the dorm, they would tell and laugh about how well their feminine wiles had worked to distract him.

In my book "FAITH TALK: a spiritual memoir inviting reflection and dialogue," I've already written about being forever grateful for the serious impact two of the professors (Dr. Paul R. Shelly and Professor Archie Perry) made at crucial turning points in my life at BC, so I'll not repeat those stories here. However, another vivid memory illustrates quite well how times have changed since the early Fifties. Miss Edna Ramseyer required all members of the Foods Class to KILL, dress, and cook a chicken. At home, we raised chickens and marketed them (fresh dressed, cut-up or whole) every weekend. I had already dressed hundreds of chickens and knew the whole process beginning at the chopping block, but Mother was always the one who cut off their heads. Pacifist that I am, I knew I couldn't kill one. I told Miss Edna that I thought it was an unreasonable request. She explained that she wanted each of her students to be prepared for the day when we would get a call from our husband's office saying he was bringing the boss home for dinner. She said we'd need to be able to fix chicken from beginning to end. So, what could any intelligent and conscientious student do? I skipped class on the day of the "big kill." Miss Edna accepted my "sick" excuse and then told me that I'd have to make up the beheading assignment. Unable to escape, I followed her out to the old

151

barn that was still on campus, put the chicken's neck between two nails in a board that was lying flat on the ground, and lifted the hatchet. As I brought it down, I sort of blacked out and hit the chicken in the back. I let loose of the chicken's legs and Miss Edna had to chase, catch, and finish killing it.

P.S. In all the years since that day, I've never owned a live chicken nor have I ever needed to kill one.

Bluffton in later years
BY RUTH NAYLOR

In the late Sixties my husband, Stan, was invited to return and work for the college. We were living in Ft. Wayne at the time, but he had always been partial to and supportive of his alma mater. Our two children, Kim and Jeff, were now in elementary school, and it seemed like the perfect opportunity for me to finish work for a bachelor's degree without losing any of the credit I'd accumulated there years earlier. Housing in Bluffton was incredibly tight. There was nothing to buy or rent. It took a whole semester before we could find a place to live, but finally the little white bungalow on the Spring Street edge of campus became available and we were blessed to rent it. Retired Professor H. W. Berky and his wife, Olga, were living next door in the lovely house that the professor and his son had built of stone from the Bluffton quarry. (It's known as the Houshower House today.) H. W. and Olga were delightful neighbors. One day, Olga told us that she had been baking and asked Kim and Jeff if they liked squash pie. They turned up their noses at the idea of *squash* pie; so, she waited until the next day to bring over what she called a *pumpkin* pie and the children loved it. H.W. taught us why the tomato plants in our little backyard garden had mysteriously died. He knew what we didn't, that the roots of the big walnut tree nearby were responsible for poisoning the plants. One day, Jeff noticed that H.W. was burying bricks under his grapevines. Jeff, who was in second grade at the time, couldn't understand why anyone would be planting bricks. He asked H.W. if he thought he could grow more bricks that way. H.W. explained that the bricks would help to hold moisture for the grapevines. He was a marvelous source of knowledge. Both of the Berkys loved to talk and I enjoyed learning from them. Whenever the three of us happened to be in their house at the same time, H.W. had a hard time getting a word in edgewise; thus, he often came over to talk when I was in the backyard. I still have to smile about the sunny summer day when H.W. came over to the lot line just as I had finished hanging out the wash. We stood there for quite a while as one story led on to another. I began to worry about his having to stand for so long a time and suggested that I get a couple of our lawn chairs so we could sit down. Considering the big difference in our ages, his response took me quite by surprise. "Oh no," he said. "I'm afraid people might talk."

Teaching at Bluffton High School
BY RUTH NAYLOR

I taught in the English Department at Bluffton High School from 1972 to 1984. I wondered how it would be to have my own children, Kim and Jeff, as students, but I felt we were pretty successful at accommodating the difference between our relationships in the classroom and at home. Both did their assignments without complaining. At least I don't remember that they complained, and I know that I made it a point not to show any favoritism. There was one time, though, that Jeff felt a bit torn between knowing me as a teacher and caring about me as his mother. At the end of one school day he came into my classroom and began with a disclaimer. "I hate the idea of ratting on anyone, but… " He hesitated and I could see that he was concerned. "There is something I think you should know." "What is it, Jeff?" I was immediately all ears. "I just don't want you to get into trouble," he explained. He hesitantly continued, "Have you noticed that (he named a couple of boys that I'm choosing not to name here) are always checking the geranium on your back windowsill when they come into class?" I admitted that I hadn't particularly noticed, and he continued. "They planted marijuana seeds in it and they check every day to see if they have started growing." Believe me, I began checking my geranium plant every day as well, but the shade it created over the whole pot must have kept the marijuana seeds at bay.

At least one other student prank succeeded. I was the Buccaneer yearbook advisor. Matt Ziessler, a senior and our staff artist in 1981, created some lovely artwork for the interior of the book and also designed the cover which features two large foaming waves on a sea of blue. If you look very closely at the white foam, you can see the words "Pink Floyd," the name of a popular singing group that some but certainly not everyone appreciated in the Eighties. After the book was published, another member of the staff told me about it. You have to look carefully for the words to see them, but they are there, part of the foam. I still don't know whether my always supportive Principal Larry Brunswick or Dr. Charles Buroker, the equally appreciative superintendent at the time, ever knew about it. There is another story involving Mr. Brunswick that I still find amusing. This happened in the autumn of 1984 after I had resigned my position at the high school and accepted a call to serve on the pastoral staff at First Mennonite Church. By then, he had been promoted to superintendent of Bluffton schools. We happened to meet on Main Street in front of Citizens National Bank. His eyes lit up when he saw me and it was obvious that he had something he wanted to say to me. Of course, I was more than ready to listen. Thus, he began: "I've been wanting to tell you something I have learned about Mennonites." I had long known that he was a Catholic so I tuned right in to see what he knew about those of us who worshipped in the big yellow-brick church at the corner of Church and Jackson Streets. "I've learned," he said, "that I should never take just one Mennonite fishing with me. If I want to take one, I always need to take at least two." He paused and his teasing smile told me that this was going to be a joke. Of course, I encouraged him to tell me why he needed to take two. He very willingly continued, "If I take just one, he'll drink all of my beer, but if I take two, neither one of them will drink." I sort of miss having my former administrators around here in Bluffton.

Nine Bluffton vignettes
BY RICK EMMERT

I – Friday, Nov. 22, 1963. I am sure many of us over a certain age can recall where we were when we heard the news of that day. At the time, Bluffton junior high classes were in the same building as the high school classes and with many of the same teachers. I was in an afternoon eighth grade history class with Mr. Bowden. The classroom door was open into a quiet hallway when Mr. Bowden looked toward the door and then quickly went over to briefly converse with a person standing there. He soon came back to report that he had just spoken with Sally Emmert, my older sister who was a senior in high school and also in one of Mr. Bowden's history classes. She had come to tell him that word had just come to the school office that President Kennedy had been assassinated. Of course, we were all shocked as was Mr. Bowden. Within a couple of minutes, Mrs. Lewis, the secretary in the office, rang the school announcement chime and then came over the PA system with the cryptic message. It went something like this: "President Kennedy has been shot in Dallas, Texas, and is now dead." Our class had minutes earlier already been surprised with that news so we were silent. But from outside in the quiet hallway we could hear a huge collective gasp which seemed to echo throughout the whole school. Then Mrs. Lewis, pausing briefly to let the news sink in or perhaps unsure if she should say something more, rang the chime again to signal the announcement was over. A historical day spent in an eighth grade history class.

II – It was a lazy summer afternoon when we were 15 years old. Though we were basically good boys, we still occasionally got up to a bit of mischief. That day, myself and a friend from the Mennonite Church did something rather un-Christian. We were exploring in the tall church belfry and climbed up to the top beside the bell from where we could peer out over Bluffton. The belfry naturally had a very good view of the Methodist Church across the street and looking down from on high we could see the 8-year-old son of the Methodist minister lolling about on the grass of the Methodist churchyard. Hiding in the shadows of the belfry, I called out in a strong yet gentle voice to the young boy who here I shall refer to as Bobby (The name has been changed to protect the innocent!). "Hey Bobby." "Who is that? Where are you?" he replied, looking around trying to find from where and whom the voice was coming. He seemed to have a sense that it was coming from atop the Mennonite Church but he could not see us so he looked up and around at the nearby trees and buildings. "Bobby, this," I asserted, "is God." "What? Who are you? Stop that!" He didn't exactly sound convinced of my words. But it was here that the deceit became a bit more, well, deceitful. "Bobby, God is a Mennonite!" Thereafter we quickly and quietly climbed back down the belfry leaving young Bobby to ponder a new perspective on religion.

III – We all had heard of the infamous robbing of the Bluffton Citizens National Bank in the summer of 1933 by the equally infamous John Dillinger. Of course, we were of the next generation so we only had the stories of our parents and our imaginations to think about what that day must have been like. Instead, we started making plans to pull off our own heist. Actually, a faux heist. Not so much to make money, but to make humor. We weren't going to do this à la the Dillinger gang but more in the realm of the Three Stooges. The plan had a number of variations. One, which I recall, developed one night while we were parked along Church Street just down from the bank. That plan was to rent a black Cadillac and at noon on a Saturday we would drive into town, park the Cadillac just there on Church Street, jump out in our '40s-era long black overcoats and stylish black fedoras, then stride purposefully up to the front door of the bank. And with fedoras pulled low in front of our eyes, we would look around menacingly as we pull on the bank's front door – only to find that it was now past noon and the bank was closed and the door was locked. We would then turn around, still maintaining are "menacingliness" and hightail it back to the car, jump in and scurry out of town before anyone recognized that we were just four high school guys. For some reason, though we spent a lot of time and laughter imagining this, we never did get around to pulling off our faux heist.

IV – A small-world story. In July 1970, I went to Japan for a junior year abroad from Earlham College. As one member of a group of 20 students from 12 Great Lakes colleges, we spent our first couple of weeks studying Japanese intensively in a Japanese inn up in the mountains near Nagano in central Japan. Midway through the course we had a day off so a number of us decided to do an overnight climb of nearby Mt. Myoko. Leaving in the late evening, we arrived at the mountaintop around daybreak and gazed at the mountain peaks that spread in the distance across the Japanese main island of Honshu. Our group made up of American students and a couple of Japanese teachers and staff was the only group at the summit until, strangely enough, a group of

157

young American high school students also arrived at the top. We paid little mind to them as we enjoyed the scenery, until suddenly I heard one of the high schoolers yell out, "Hey, Ramseyer!" Now, my parents had told me about Bob and Alice Ruth Ramseyer who were based on the southern island of Kyushu serving as Mennonite missionaries. But that was way far away. I made my way over to the high school group and enquired. Sure enough, one of the boys was Mark Ramseyer, son of Bob and Alice Ruth. It turns out that nearby was a popular campground used by missionaries from all over Japan, and Mark and his friends were spending summer vacation there. Later, during my year in Japan, I went to visit the Ramseyers in Kyushu. Mark went on to be a professor of Japanese law at Harvard University. But I certainly didn't expect to hear a Bluffton name at the summit of a mountain in Japan.

V – In 1976, I was in graduate school in Tokyo while my brother Jan was working on a Ph.D. at the University of Michigan by spending a couple of years in Bangladesh doing research. In February-March, the long spring break in my school year, I flew from Tokyo to Dacca to visit my brother and we traveled around both Bangladesh and India for six weeks. Jan's research had taken him to several towns and villages throughout Bangladesh and I went with him to visit a couple of these, both of which he had extensively visited previously. These two visits for me were most notable because of two food-related episodes. The first was at a village where all the elders gathered to greet the American researcher they had gotten to know as he studied their village. We were welcomed with a rather large evening dinner celebration which featured a delicious chicken curry. Jan was treated with great respect. So much so that he was offered the special delicacy always given to the most respected person in attendance – the chicken head which had also been cooked well in the curry. Jan clearly had experience with all of this and since he was only in his 30s, he could easily demur and suggest that one of the elders be given the delicacy instead. His gracious act pleased everyone as it showed how the young researcher paid respect to the village elders. Later on Jan revealed to me that the act was not entirely altruistic – he was absolutely not fond of eating chicken heads. Jan is presently the age of those elders, and I wonder what would happen if he went back to visit that village now. I kind of think he would somehow have to buck up and partake of that chicken head. The second food episode took place soon after at a bigger town. Jan and I arrived at night and stayed at a small inn. Early the next morning I went with him as he made the rounds of meeting various people he was particularly close to, speaking in Bengali and translating for me. We first met the town mayor who immediately ordered delicious chai tea with a rich Bengali sweet. I had already learned that Bengali sweets were not only very flavorful but also very, very sweet, and of course I thoroughly enjoyed it. An hour or so later we went on to meet yet another friend who did the same thing, i.e. quickly ordered chai and another amazing Bengali sweet which we ate again. And then soon after we visited yet another friend, and yes, it happened again and this time I remember that I ate that sweet a bit more slowly than the earlier ones. And now it was a little before noon in the Bangladesh heat of midday, and I was beginning to get a rather uncomfortable sugar high. But Jan needed to visit one more home and we walked across some fields with a number of deep small ponds on both sides of the path. These ponds acted as reservoirs during the hot dry season. This time we visited the home of a young couple who obviously were quite poor and did not have the means to order a fancy sweet. Jan, of course, insisted that nothing was necessary, but they still wanted to show their hospitality by providing something for their guests. I could see into the kitchen as the wife put sugar in a cheesecloth and whisked it around in water, and soon we were provided with some very sweet sugar water. I quietly said to Jan that I didn't think I could handle any more sweet of any kind but he encouraged me to drink just a little to not embarrass our hosts. I did drink some, perhaps half a glass full and we soon took our leave. On the way back I was beginning to sway with the sugar racing through my veins and the heat on my brow, and as we walked the narrow path, I was sure I was going to slip into one of the ponds. Somehow we wound our way through the ponds and back to our inn where the host had prepared lunch. By that time, I was in no shape to eat anything but could only lie down which I did for the rest of the day. Somehow I managed to sleep off the sugar high. Two Bluffton brothers in a distant land – one who could not hold his sugar!

VI – In the fall of 1964, I was a lowly freshman in high school playing saxophone in Miss Souder's marching band, the product of her initiative from the previous year, which we affectionately called "sax lessons" to train some of the clarinet players to play saxophone during the fall marching band season to give the band a stronger sound. We would then switch back to clarinet during the concert band season. Several weeks into our rigorous marching band season, the senior bass drummer had a dispute with Miss Souder and suddenly quit the band. We were left without that important role whose forceful beat basically kept the band together as we marched through our various formations. For some reason, I was asked to take on this role. Unlike now, at that time I was quite slim and thought there must be someone who would be more solidly built who could carry that heavy bass drum. Why was I chosen, I wondered? Maybe I wasn't that good a saxophone player. Likely there were others who could have done the job but were more valuable than me at their own instruments. In any case, I was tasked with the job and somehow proved strong enough to carry both the drum and the beat. Though our performances were usually at Pirate football games on Friday night, one Saturday afternoon we were asked to play the halftime show at the Bluffton College Beavers' home game at Harmon Field. The bass drum is of course two-sided so it is played alternatively with sticks in both hands. The drummer needs to play the strokes with both hands equally strong. In the midst of that Beavers' halftime show suddenly my right hand drumstick broke. There I was forced to play what had been a beat going back and forth from right hand to left hand now all with my left hand. I somehow was able to get the good remaining drumstick into my stronger right hand without destroying the rhythm of the entire band and managed to play the rest of the show with that hand. But it wasn't easy as my right hand tired with the extra work, and I soon realized that my right hand knuckles were occasionally hitting the drumhead. When we finally got off the field, I could see that blood from my knuckles had been spattered across the drumhead. I wiped off what I could but the following week noticed that there remained a small but noticeable dried patch of blood on the drumhead. It stayed there for the rest of the season. The following year I was back to playing saxophone and clarinet. But occasionally I looked at the bass drum and realized that the blood patch remained. In fact it remained up through my senior year. I've always wondered if anyone eventually washed off my DNA from that drumhead. And I sometimes wonder if it could possibly still be there 50 years later?

VII – During the summer of 1967 before our senior year of high school, I was able to convince my father to let me borrow the family VW so close friends Jim Heiks, Phil Yost and I could take a two-week trip up into Canada. During the trip Jim would also share the driving responsibilities with me while Phil, as yet unlicensed, mainly did the navigating. Our trip took us up to Toronto where I had spent three weeks the previous summer, and on to Montreal where we spent a couple of days at Expo 67. We even went further up to Quebec City hoping to meet some pretty French girls our age, but truth be told, we failed miserably at that. I think our French was just not good enough... or something! Still we had a wonderful time as we came back into the States through Maine to Boston where I had cousins, and then across Massachusetts and New York and eventually safely back home to Bluffton. Before leaving, my Dad had warned me that there could possibly be an occasional starter problem with the VW and, if that happened, he taught me how to pop the clutch while the car was being pushed in gear in order to get it started again. Sure enough, part way during the trip the starter began to fail us although not consistently until we were crossing upstate New York. Each time this happened, since I was the only one who felt confident about the clutch-popping trick, Jim and Phil would have to push the car with me in the driver's seat and I would pop the clutch and we would be off. On Interstate 90, Jim was driving with Phil in the front passenger seat and me barefooted in the back seat. We were outside of Buffalo in late afternoon just in time for the rush hour which slowed the traffic to a snail's pace. In the midst of starts and stops in three-lane traffic, sure enough, Jim stalled the car. It was suddenly "Chinese fire drill" time. Jim and Phil jumped out of the front seats and went around to the back of the car. I jumped out barefooted from the back seat and got into the driver's seat. Fortunately the clutch was successfully popped and the car started, Jim and Phil got back in, and duly embarrassed we continued on our journey with me barefoot at the wheel.

VIII – Shaking hands with a great man! In June 1965, my cousin graduated from Antioch College in Yellow Springs, Ohio, and I went down to his commencement ceremony because Martin Luther King Jr., whose wife Coretta Scott King had graduated from Antioch, was giving the commencement address.

MLK of course was widely known and was certainly the most visible spokesperson and leader in the Civil Rights Movement of the late '50s and the '60s. I knew MLK had his detractors even around Bluffton and I remember that was evident among some of my classmates who made what I considered some very disparaging remarks about him after he was assassinated three years later. But I was a big admirer of Dr. King and his cause and thought this was my chance to be in the presence of the great man who was still only in his mid-30s. The ceremony was held outside and I listened to the speech from the very back of the audience. At the end of the ceremony, it was announced that MLK and his wife would be meeting audience members at the side of the stage. I took advantage of my being at the very back of the audience to race way around the side of the audience, and was thus able to be the second or third in line to meet him. In awe, I shook hands with him and he smiled at me and said something like, "Thank you, son." And that was it. But it made my day, my year and perhaps my life. As I wrote this piece, I looked up online anything about MLK's visit to Antioch. I was surprised to see that the Dayton Daily News revealed a year after the speech that there had been a KKK plan to assassinate MLK as he spoke at Antioch. Several gunmen were involved and they also planned to fire into the audience to disrupt the entire proceedings. The plan was reportedly cancelled about 10 days before MLK's speech.

IX – Swiss Day. In May 1968, several of us got together to practice some German band music that we planned to perform at the annual Swiss Day luncheon to be held down on the Bluffton College baseball green. Fred Steiner played trombone, Jim Heiks was on French horn, Ken Graber was on baritone and I played clarinet. Fred, Jim and I were all soon to graduate and we assumed that it would be no problem for us to miss several classes at school to go down and play for the noon event taking place on a school day. But our first request for this resulted in a clear "no" from our principal, Walter Marshall. I remember thinking that this was grossly unfair. It was spring and every day saw the baseball team or the track team being excused an hour before classes ended to get ready for games and meets to take place after school. Here we were about to graduate, had good grades and though we weren't athletes, we were musicians asking only for a couple hours off. Mr. Marshall's office was in a room to the left side of the main school office counter. To the right side of the counter was the office of the school guidance counselor who just happened to be my father, Paul Emmert. Our little band regrouped and marched into the office and once more asked to see Mr. Marshall. I noticed that the guidance counselor's door was open, which suggested he was in and could certainly hear us. Mr. Marshall came out and again we stated our request and were given excuses why this would be a bad example to the rest of the school. We made our case forcefully bringing up how the three of us were soon to graduate, how the athletes were quite often let out of school early and what we were asking for was really not much. Mr. Marshall resisted, but finally we wore him down and he said we could go. We said thank you and smugly walked out. That night when I got home my father just smiled broadly when he saw me and said nothing.

Raising a boy near the banks of the Riley
BY A BLUFFTON MOM

There was nothing better than growing up near the banks of the Riley. My son delivered newspapers and knew every inch of town by the time he was 12... and he thought he owned it all. He and a friend knew where to find scrap lumber to build a raft to float down the Riley. I only found out about it because they hit a log jam at the Fett Road bridge and their long walk home made him late for supper. I had an errand to run in Lima and hurried home before school was out. As I turned onto our street I was horrified to see a fire truck in our driveway with puffs of smoke coming out of our garage. Several firemen were in full gear. I rushed to see what was happening and found the firemen doubled over with laughter. Unbeknownst to me, my son and his friend found a way to get up on boards in the crawl space of our garage. The firemen discovered they were rolling their own cigarettes and looking at Playboy magazines in their wonderful hide-away.

My son eventually grew up, became employed, got married and had a son of his own to challenge him. He's not divorced, isn't in jail, isn't on drugs and hasn't moved back home. Life is good.

Bluffton flashback

BY CAROLYN URICH RICH

I had a flashback the other day when driving down Bluffton's Main Street. I was in the Green Hornet (our 1957 Nash) and pulling into the D&E Sinclair station at the corner of Main and College Avenue, where our public library now stands. As I pulled up to the gas pump, Dean Nonnamaker, with a big smile on his face, ran out to the car before I could roll down the window. I said, "Fill'er up," and while asking about the kids he was not only filling the gas tank, but washing the windows, lifting the hood to check the oil and kicking the tires to make sure the pressure was okay. I handed him a five dollar bill and my loyalty was sealed before he could bring back the change. Now that was service! I could have gone to the Phillips station across the street, Bucher's SOHIO station, Renner's (earlier there was Stauffer's) Pure Oil station, two Marathon stations (Hardwick's and Brooke's); Cookson was a Marathon distributor and Triplehorn, a SOHIO distributor), but Dean's friendly smile kept me coming back.

In the 1950s and '60s Bluffton's businessmen earned your loyalty because they all had competition. There were choices of places to spend your money. There were at least two of all the

165

necessary businesses to thrive: groceries (Urich's IGA Foodliner, A&P, Art Amstutz Grocery, City Market, Community Market, Clover Farm Market, Stager's Grocery, and later the Imperial Discount Grocery), two hardwares (Fett and Greding), two men's clothing stores (Geiger and Diller, Steiner and Huser), women's clothing stores (Balmer's, Rice Dry Goods became Reistman's became Jan's, and Vida-Vidella), a department store (The Charles Company) two jewelers (Ernsberger and Leiber's), Lantz's Gift Shop, Waltermire's General Store (run by the first Bluffton woman entrepreneur), drug stores (Skelly's, Millager's, and Hauenstein, which became Loofbourrow's Rexall), three lumber companies (Reichenbach, Steinman Bros. and Garmatter), plumbers (Reignbuhler, which became M&R, and Hauenstein), car dealers (Bob Williams Chevrolet Co., Brooke Motor Sales, Bixel Motor Sales), and C.F. Niswander & Son sold International Harvester tractors, implements and trucks. We even had two funeral homes (Diller and Basinger).

Your relatives, friends you went to church with or who lived in your neighborhood, often determined your loyalty. Speaking of churches, Sunday mornings and evenings our village separated in groups of Methodists, Presbyterians, Lutherans, three or four different Mennonite congregations, Missionary, United Church of Christ, Church of Christ, Catholic and Christian Scientist. Some have since closed. You had a choice of four doctors (Rodabaugh, Shelly, Travis and Soash) and a couple dentists (Francis and Evan Basinger and later Huss). We had one optometrist (Bixel, and later Yoder), but Travis would check your eyes, too. Niswander and Herring were our vets, followed by Benner. And we had our very own Bluffton Community Hospital. There were plenty of places to get food: Basinger's Meat Market, Swanks Bros. Meat Market, A to Z Meat Market and Locker Service, a bakery (Hauenstein's, bought out by Gillett's), a carry-out (Kibbies), places to get wonderful ice cream (Hankish's and Benroth's Dari-Delite). Montgomery's (later bought out by Lugibihl) sold ice cream at their newsstand on North Main. Restaurants included Pine Restaurant, later bought by Martz and Ingalls, who built Ingalls restaurant across the alley, Edelweiss Restaurant, the Horseshoe Grill (with the seating area shaped like a horseshoe), Stoney's Bar, Anderson's Buckeye Lunch (by the swimming pool, which became Das Winkler Haus and later the Strawberry Patch), and Joe's Pizza (purchased from Mast). Residents knew which farmers to go to for produce and meat to can or freeze and take to the A to Z or locker in nearby Pandora. We had our very own newspaper, the Bluffton News, Niswander's Newsstand, Basinger Furniture Store, a bank (Citizens National) worthy of the infamous Dillinger gang robbery, Crow's (where you could buy just about anything for 5 cents to $1.00), Rice Dry Goods, Hilty's Flowers and Rammel's. There was Boehr Realty, Sylvia Garmatter Real Estate and Jones Realty. Farmer's Grain Co., with its building still standing on Cherry Street, attracted long lines of tractors with trailers at harvest time. (If those lines weren't long, there would be long lines at the bank, according to newsman Chuck Hilty). Their competition was Bluffton Milling Co. Other businesses were Augsburger's Garage, Koontz Sinclair Service, Western Auto Store, Master Mix Feed Mill, Gable's Painting Service, and numerous insurance agents (including Leland Diller, Clarence Diller, A.C. Burcky, and Bruce Shelly), barbers (Patterson, Swank, Smith and Johnson) and beauticians (Chamberlain, and others working out of their homes). We had a professional photographer (Gerber). There was Alspach Cleaners, Sutie's Cleaners, Econo-Wash and Dixie Marathon Service & Laundry. We not only had Gratz shoe store (where you could see your bones in the X-ray machine), and also a shoe repairman, Doc Ludwig. Page Dairy was on Harmon Road, often leaving the Riley Creek looking milky. Noah Steiner's stockyard was located on Vance Street. Herr Gardens served our gardening needs. Postmasters were Ed Reichenbach, Ralph Sterns and Woodrow Little. Our mailman, Ralph Reichenbach, refinished antiques. Need chicks? There was Amstutz Hatcheries and Jorg Hatchery. The Moon-Winx Motel was located a few miles out of town where Richland Manor Nursing Home was located. In addition to the Big and Little Riley Creeks, which could become rivers in times of floods, we had two big bodies of water (the Buckeye quarry and the National quarry). Central Ohio Light and Power (Woodcock plant), located at the north end of the quarry, burned lots of coal, leaving dust all over town.

There were factories offering employment: Triplett Corp., Ex-Cell-O, Precision Thermoplastics Components, Bluffton Slaw Cutter, Peerless Glove Corp., Bluffton Farm Equipment, and Bluffton Stone Co. Another big employer was Bluffton College, established in 1900.

There was plenty of entertainment in our little village of 2,300-3,000 residents in the 1950s-'60s. We had a swimming pool, a bowling alley (Southgate Lanes) and Bluffton Golf Course. There were clay tennis courts. These were well maintained by Wilbur Howe, a high school teacher, who for 16 years was mayor. And to top it off, we had a movie theatre (Star and later Carma) with good popcorn and a movie for only 50 cents. Bluffton had a lot to celebrate on its centennial in 1961. Yes, Bluffton was a thriving town, with constant traffic cruising down Main Street coming from Dayton and Lima in the south and heading to Findlay and Toledo to the north. Bluffton's residents did most of their shopping in town, only venturing out for a Christmas shopping treat.

In 1955 we began exploring the world beyond us. A Denny's Restaurant eventually appeared at the 103-Intersate 75 exit. Better paying jobs enticed us to Lima and Findlay. More reliable cars lured us further from home for entertainment and shopping. North/south traffic bypassed us without stopping.

The Greyhound bus no longer stopped here, nor did the Nickel Plate Railroad stop on the way to Cleveland and Buffalo in the morning or to Frankfort, Indiana, and branching off to St. Louis in the evening. The number of freight trains dwindled. Gradually the business district changed to adapt to the times. Many villages would die under these circumstances, but the Bluffton community spirit, ingenuity and people continue to thrive... leaving us with wonderful memories of the "good old days" of the 1950s and '60s.

The quarry test
BY RICK RAMSEYER

All these years later, I still remember the dread I felt before taking the quarry test. This wasn't a written exam, and it had nothing to do with school. It was a rite of passage for any Bluffton kid from around the mid-1950s to the early-1990s who wanted to earn the right to swim in Buckeye quarry – better known as simply the Buckeye or the quarry – rather than in the town swimming pool directly beside it. The quarry test consisted of a what seemed like a 50-yard swim from the large concrete deck on the southeastern edge of the Buckeye to a wooden raft and then back again, accompanied by a lifeguard. The expectation was to keep swimming, with no dog paddling allowed, though you could rest briefly when you reached the raft. If you stopped along the way you failed the test – an all-too public failure magnified by living in a small town where pretty much everyone knew each other, or at least it seemed that way to me. But passing the test was a badge of honor, an indication that you too could walk down the wide set of steps to the Buckeye to join the older kids for bigger adventures and all that came with it: three diving boards – low, medium and high – a metal slide and two rafts that served as tiny islands to chat with friends and watch the bustle on shore. In the mid-1950s, well before the current swimming complex was constructed along

Snider Road, Bluffton built a small community pool probably 30 yards from the southeastern end of the quarry, where a park now is. The pool was a good option for a cool dip on a muggy August afternoon, but the distinctive thunk-thunk of the diving boards and the excited shrieks of swimmers shooting down the slide into the Buckeye made the pool seem far less attractive – a place for little kids, parents and grandparents. Even then, the Buckeye had a long history as a favorite swimming spot. About a quarter mile long and maybe half a football field across at its widest point, it originally was the site of a limestone quarry that ceased operations in the 1890s. Fed by a spring with water that's best described as murky, it became a popular place to swim and fish. (The Bluffton Sportsmen's Club has stocked the Buckeye for decades and has held its annual trout derby there for nearly 80 years.)

I'm not sure how old I was when I took the quarry test – maybe 10 or 11 – and I don't remember who the lifeguard was. I have a vivid memory of standing on the concrete deck, my heart hammering as I jumped in, my body briefly shocked by the cold water. I wasn't a strong swimmer, but I'd taken lessons at the community pool. Swimming slowly and steadily, the lifeguard beside me with a ring buoy, I passed the test with a sense of pride and relief.

From then on, throughout my early teens, summer afternoons were often spent at the Buckeye, swimming and sliding and diving with friends, the scent of suntan lotion in the air and a parade of pop music playing over loudspeakers. It's been years since I've lived in Bluffton, and sometimes when I return to visit I drive to the parking lot beside the China Wok restaurant on North Main Street and get out to look around. The old community pool is long gone, and the Buckeye isn't open to swimming anymore. But in the distance it still beckons, a place where hundreds, probably thousands, of Bluffton kids swam on many a summer day. The price of entry? A simple test to prove you belonged. As I look back on those days, the quarry test really wasn't that hard, though passing it clearly seemed to matter. I see now it represented something else: a small step, a modest milestone, on the journey to growing up.

Living where we live
BY JEFF GUNDY

What have I done to deserve such a life? That seems the question, these slow summer days. There's the constant rumbling of misery and disaster, the thunderstorms of even greater and more concentrated miseries brought daily by the papers and the radio and the TV news. There's the chorus of warnings about slower but even more drastic calamities bearing down on us, asteroids already inside the orbit of Jupiter. Here I am in the midst of it all, sitting in my warm office with the fan buzzing, reading idly in the latest Georgia Review and a copy of The Norton Book of Friendship that a friend gave me on her way out of town, trying to decide whether I should feel privileged or deprived.

This noon, with our oldest son away at music camp, our middle one at a friend's, and the youngest at the sitter's, my wife and I had a quiet, pleasant lunch alone at home – sandwiches with leftover chicken from last night and endive from the garden, broccoli, carrots, iced tea. She went back to work and I came back here, not knowing what I'd do, nothing in the world I have to do before 3:30, when I'm to meet a friend for handball. It'll be hot and sweaty, I'll lose two games as I almost always do, pound the walls and yell at myself for my stupidity and lack of killer instinct.

Afterwards my partner and I will talk academic politics and sports until we start to cool down, and then I'll go home to the air conditioning and sit around the rest of the evening, read, and feel self-righteous for working out in the middle of the heat. Tomorrow will be more or less the same. Next week, if I can work up the gumption, I mean to replace the broken shingles on the garage – basketball damage on the front side, soccer on the back – and paint it.

It's not a hard life. It seems insane or at least immodest to complain about it. On the farm where I was raised we were led to believe that while we Mennonites were as good as anybody, and in our very humility better than most, we shouldn't expect that the ordinary folk would ever realize it. We were led to think, as William Stafford says in his wonderful, loopy poem about midwestern expectations, that God would be proud of us if we could just stay out of jail. If we got through college and found steady jobs, why, he'd probably let us into heaven just for not being a burden on the welfare system.

None of this was ever said directly or out loud, of course. Mennonites, at least when they're acting most like Mennonites, don't say much directly unless it's about the weather or farming or it comes directly from the Bible or the hymnal. The Swiss-German stock I come from, in particular, has centuries of farming in its blood, and so it seems quite natural that my father has a keen grasp of the quirks and fundamental irrationalities of midwestern rainfall and the Chicago Board of Trade. He has tried to explain what he knows to me more than once, mainly without success. This may be because I've left the old ways, found work that allows me to stay out of the summer sun, keep my hands clean and soft, and get paychecks that go a whole year without changing a penny. I've always thought of myself as the wild one of the family, but in a month I will have been living in the same house in Bluffton for 10 full years. In those ways, even though my work is different, my life is not so different from my parents' and their parents, who lived in their own small farm communities just a few hundred miles west.

My wife has never lived this long in one house before. I have, in the old farm house my parents moved into just after I was born, where we lived until I was 14. Then we built the new house, in an L-shape around the old one, and they still live in it. We've been in this house long enough to be starting on the second round of redecorating: a few summers ago we did the kitchen for the second time, digging deeper this time, moving the washer and drier, buying better linoleum that doesn't show the dirt. The cabinet handles and drawer pulls we bought the first time – white porcelain with brass bolts – are in the basement in a butter dish, still plenty good, waiting for somebody to need them.

Mainly we like it where we are, in this village with 4,000 people, mainly white, mainly Republican, mainly church-goers. The Mennonites have the biggest church, but are still a minority. We can tick off all the advantages for the friends and prospects that come through: the quiet streets, the new pool our kids can get to on their bikes, the little hospital, the dollar theater downtown. Two large drinks and a big tub of popcorn are still only four bucks. The school has ambitious parents for miles around trying to wedge their kids into it, though some of us suspect the test scores are high just because of all the professors' kids. For the children there are soccer and baseball and choir and strings and piano, not to mention pick-up games of street hockey and football and kick the can, and the friends they bring home seem occasionally rowdy but not seriously delinquent. Some afternoons they disappear for hours, come home a little breathless and scratched up to tell about their adventures wandering in the patch of woods along Little Riley Creek, the hollow tree they call the Nose Hideout, or their failed efforts to dam the creek.

Still, on these summer days it's hard to escape that old small-town yearning, that suspicion that real life must be someplace else. A few weeks ago a friend from the big city stopped by with her husband, whom we'd never met. These people are so hip they don't even own a car. They go to dinner parties with people whose names are on the mastheads of magazines. He has a burr haircut, the kind I had in fourth grade and will go to my grave before I have again. He collects old records by people like Doris Day and Dean Martin, the kind my parents got a whole clump of with their first, blonde console stereo 30 years ago. He actually claims to listen to them, and to like them.

I thought Doris Day was smarmy and ridiculous even 30 years ago, when we'd sit around and play those records on summer afternoons, singing along mockingly, waving our arms in the air. It was a whole different thing when the Beatles made it onto the radio – they were *serious*, yeah, yeah, yeah. But now I'm forced to wonder if I missed something in that whole "Que sera, sera" business. Are my CD's by R.E.M. and the Indigo Girls just another symptom of my hapless small-town midbrow cultural ineptitude, my inability to recognize what's *really* cool? Never mind Dylan and Neil Young. Never mind Paul Simon, even if he is a New Yorker. I don't admit any of this to David, of course, and he's politely quiet, a maneuver I'm pretty good at myself when I know I have an edge.

They tell us how they visited another small-town acquaintance and he actually *showed them the college.* They hoot. What is with these people, they say. We don't tell them that when people come to see us, usually, we show them the college. It's just a couple of blocks away, it makes a nice stroll after breakfast or lunch, and it's not like the other choices are the Brooklyn Bridge or the Metropolitan Museum. Besides, the campus looks pretty good these days. There's the new art building, the dorm going up, and the new statue. We had a contest for the statue, with big bucks for the winner, by our standards anyway, five figures. We got money from the Arts Council and applications from all over. The first round looked wonderful, but when it got right down to it we had our doubts about all three of the finalists. One was a lion with lamb that was too sentimental and gauche even for us, one had cutouts of children with sharp edges everywhere for the kids to fall and hurt themselves on. But what could we do by then? We're sensitive about our artistic sophistication or lack of, but finally we went for the one that was sort of symbolic and not obviously dangerous. So we ended up with three polished slabs of granite, with some rough rocks in a semi-circle around them. There's a story attached, something about three warring African chiefs getting together to Work It Out Peacefully by sitting on these three rocks. It's the kind of stuff I've heard painters and sculptors say about their work before; it always makes me think that either they've invented it all afterward, or they were born with very good hands but incredibly simple ideas. Peace Thrones, that's the title, but the word around town was, did you hear how much the college paid for three chunks of granite? Some of the students were all up in arms, thinking it came out of their tuition money, though it didn't.

But we have the statue now, and one way or another it's paid for, and anyway it's half-hidden on the edge of the woods and a person can walk around for months and never really notice it. I still haven't quite made up my own mind; I keep telling myself I have to go sit on a throne for a half-hour sometime and see if I start thinking peaceable thoughts. But a few weeks ago something shifted me toward hope, one more time. There was an opening in the art gallery, and one of our friends had some paintings there with a friend of hers, a sculptor from Chicago. Her daughter, our youngest son Joel, and some other kids had run off quickly, bored with grown-ups holding glasses of sticky punch (no booze on campus), gazing at watercolor fish and faces assembled out of old tools and rusty wire. When I went looking for the kids I found them down the hill, at the new sculpture. They were jumping from stone to stone in a circle, all five of them, going round and round, the little girls with their good dresses swinging, my son among them in his shorts and t-shirt, 10 arms waving for balance.

175

Some were trying to go fast as they could, passing the others at the slightest chance, others just kept stepping round and round, making the easy jump from stone to stone in a steady rhythm.

I walked down to them. Close up I heard them talking, more or less constantly, without stopping the procession. Somebody wanted to go home, somebody wanted to swim, somebody was mad because she'd fallen. But they kept going round, they barely noticed me there even when I tried to talk to them, ask them what they were doing – as if I didn't know. They didn't explain; they just kept going round, as if they were on some business, some ritual that did not require silence or perfection but that needed to be completed. I tried to tell Joel that we were going home. The first two times he pretended not to hear me. The third time he said he wanted to stay with his friends, that they were playing, and couldn't he come home when they were done, later. It's just a block, after all. And because we live where we live, I could say yes.

Thread
if my life is a thread being pulled by a needle . . .
If the chimes of freedom flash like the flash that caught you
half a mile from home last night, still circling the quarry,

wondering suddenly where the ducks and geese find shelter . . .
All you knew was to keep going, let the needle in your head

pull you onward, sweaty and puffing again, lucky, keeping
the pace you can, almost too fast, hoping to get lost in the music

or your worries and forget for a while the labor and sweat
and small pains, heel, knee, ankle, the swing of arm, thud,

thud on pavement, just keep on, follow the pull toward
the next turn, the next familiar street, forget the thunder

or wait for it after the flash, feel the breeze and know the storm
will find you if it chooses, wind in your face or not, let it go,

the rain is cool and the shirt is wet already with your hot sweat,
too late to slow down, too soon to think of home, cross

the steel bridge and take the little rise up Spring Street, pass
the small familiar homes like a silent crowd, like people sleeping

in the pews, left on Elm to the Catholic church, good people
filing in to sing and pray but you must go on, right on Lawn,

you know what pulls you now, you know this last long street,
the time is good, the legs are weary but they bear you on,

your heart is firm and strong, the air sweeps in and out
of your open, deep, and secret lungs and somehow still

your blood takes what it needs and gives the rest away.

The Poet Watches His Neighborhood
Those who didn't mow yesterday are mowing today.

A little of the corn is yellow and feeble from standing in water too
long, but the rest is jungle-lush, eight feet tall, full of juice.

The neighbor's granddaughter has ridden her bike all day on a short
loop that includes part of my driveway. She must be bored to tears.

This morning three girls walked by in tennis gear and the prettiest one kicked the junk paper somebody throws on the sidewalk every Monday. Every Tuesday I toss it into the recycle bin still in its plastic bag, though now I hear that the bags gum up recycling equipment.

It's another mild afternoon, inexplicable for August.

I don't have a gun or a cell phone or a sense of danger, but I suppose I'm on neighborhood watch.

I failed completely at protecting Trayvon Martin.

After the verdict, my friend scolded her white friends for expressing less Facebook outrage than her black friends.

Our new grandchild is pudgy and cute beyond belief, and won't let his parents sleep more than two hours straight.

I have been failing at outrage for forty years, riding my bike in wide circles on the square roads around my town, through the numb acres of corn and soybeans and wheat stubble, the rare woodlots, crossing the creeks which are full of muddy water this year.

I wear my helmet and my biking shorts and my moisture-wicking shirt, I look in my little mirror for cars roaring up from behind. I check my speed and mileage on the quarter-sized device I got online for ten bucks, keep the time on my watch.

For an old guy I'm pretty fast: ten miles today in 33 minutes.

Not much wind, a good bike, no traffic to speak of. I got home sweaty and satisfied, needing to start dinner.

At the swinging bridge I took a break, but the mosquitos drove me away.

Two dogs at one place, but they didn't try to cross the big ditch. An old steel windmill, torn down except for the bottom eight feet of the frame.

A billboard near the interstate, facing away from the county road.

Then I sat on the screen porch with a glass of cold water and a towel. The neighbor girl was still doing laps on her bike. She only glanced at me when I tried to say hello.

Two long-haired kids on skateboards rattled by, and a girl with her little brother. Some SUVs and little Hondas.

Quarter to six. Turkey brats for the grill, fresh sweet corn, squash, tomatoes from the garden. Trayvon is still dead, his killer still free. Most nights we remember to lock our doors.

All the ground is still standing, with no help from me.

Ode with Winter Sunshine, One Mind, Four Houses
The winter birds, pleased by the sun.
Snow pushed off some of the sidewalks,

packed flat and slick on the rest,
minor ruts and chunks on the side streets.

The big red house, the little white house,
the yellow brick house and the red brick house

all seem delighted to have made it this far,
mainly intact, furnaces roaring quietly

in their cellars, shingles locked
in place, doors mostly latched.

The houses might be saying
We have ridden out another night,

and that seems strange and hopeful
when once again the streets are

passable if not clear, the walks
are passable if not clear, and a little man

in a long blue coat wanders by,
a little late as always, snug in his jeans

and boots and sweater, his mind
passable, passable if not clear.

Ohio, or Some Things Resisting Full Disclosure

Do you have any idea how exotic this place is, my friend from
California demanded?

I suppose I do, I answered in the Ohio fashion, meaning Tell me
more, meaning Convince me, meaning Not much surprises us.

She just kept looking and talking, the chain link fence along the
bike path, the teddy bear store on Main Street with 2 x 10's bracing its
walls – the snow broke a roof beam, though we think it can be fixed.

The back yards all garden and grass, too hot or cold to inhabit
most of the year.

The gray cat on the sidewalk just off the state route, splayed in one last, almost graceful plea. It'll be gone tomorrow, I said, as if that helped.

Vegetation without irrigation, streets empty in the middle of the week, and clouds so bored they wait around for days, just in case.

Cold yellow sun through black branches.

Girl running, one arm swinging loose, toward the door and her warm room.

Two toy collies in a backyard on Bentley Road, one barking at me and at the other one.

We looked at a house when we moved to town, long ago. Two women were living there, with two collies, and they told us they were moving to a house on Bentley. We haven't seen them since.

The six red cabbages my neighbors planted, then ignored.

The big fleshy leaves lay flat against the dirt through weeks of drought.

When it rained at last, somehow they lifted up, and even grew a little.

Their heads like purple baseballs, stunted and alive in the first snow.

New ice lacing the creek stones, a map of delicate elevations and relations.

Twenty-five years in the same house.

New collie.

Afterthoughts

This is a book of Bluffton oral history. Storytelling is in our village DNA and Bluffton has a history of great storytellers. Bluffton's early stories were told in Swiss dialect, then translated to English by "Hans" Jacob Schaeublin, a colorful character and a voice in the Swiss settlement. His readers loved reading his humorous column published in the early years of the Bluffton News.

Our study of Bluffton is largely affected by our own growing up here during the Eisenhower Era. Rudi, now of Homewood, Illinois, graduated from Bluffton High School in 1961 and from Bluffton College in 1967. Fred graduated from Bluffton High School in 1968, attended Bluffton College his freshman year then transferred to Bowling Green State University, where he majored in journalism, graduating in 1972.

We come from our own line of storytellers. Our mother, Margaret Steiner, and grandfather, Fred Hahn, mastered the craft. Some even accused them of being liars, but in Bluffton everyone loves a good lie with a twist of fabrication and a bit of exaggeration, told by someone who can pull it off successfully.

Beyond our own family experience, we learned much from those on both sides of the Riley. We observed town geniuses – characters who thought they owned Main Street – to those holding academic letters. Immersing ourselves in the richness of small-town life, we participated in Bluffton rodeo parades, witnessed the Bluffton Beavers master all challengers, particularly Ohio Northern and Findlay, during the Elbert Dubenion, Willie Taylor, Bill Ramseyer and Spike Berry football era. We heard and memorized the many first-hand accounts of John Dillinger's visit to Bluffton and knew where to find the bullet holes left behind after he exited the bank.

We scavenged Main Street, observing people and collecting their stories. We hauled home vintage apothecary bottles from pharmacies, naked manakins from Lape's Dry Goods, discarded paper of all sizes from the Bluffton News and countless furniture boxes from Basinger's Furniture Store, which became the forts and hideouts for the kids on Lawn Avenue. We furthered the study of the Bluffton human condition with Rudi working through college at Basinger Funeral Home, and earlier washing windows, taking out trash and sweeping floors at The Charles Company and the Vida-Vidella

Shop. Fred honed his local instincts sacking groceries at Urich's IGA Foodliner. Without these varied experiences this book otherwise would never have existed.

Most, but not all essays in this collection took place in the second half of the 20th century. Some are remembered correctly; some remembered the way we wished it happened. Following the publication of "Bluffton a Good Place to Miss" in 2011, Rudi developed the idea for this book: a book about this place in the 1950s. He titled it "Bluffton Forever." The book cover copied the 1952 Bluffton High School Buccaneer cover, a pirate in a television screen. Both title and cover significance are lost today. Everyone who attended BHS from 1950 to 1959 knows by heart the words to the school fight song, "Bluffton Forever... we will sing to thee." The pirate in the TV screen represented the decade perfectly. In this golden age of TV, 1952 was the year television advertising leaped past radio advertising, marking the new age.

Like many great ideas, we ran out of gas. Last year while visiting our sister, Mary, in Milwaukee – her version of the '50s is so dark we feared inviting her to contribute to this project – Fred came across a book titled "Milwaukee Anthology." It contains dozens of short essays about that city. Taking that idea, we merged "Bluffton Forever" into "Bluffton Anthology." And, we contacted several writers who knew a good Bluffton story to share. A nudge from the late Robert Kreider created our subtitle. We placed our "Bluffton Forever" material in this book's beginning, changing it to "What me – worry?" At the suggestion of David Rempel Smucker, we dropped in several short essays written by Fred. Then, added icing to the project with the collection of essays from our invited Bluffton guest writers.

Not all of our Bluffton stories made it into this volume. Maybe there's another book that will include Buck Schifke's version of what happened one night. Maybe the world will realize Elvis did stop here. We hope you enjoyed this anthology because we know you, too, have a Bluffton story to share. Your story may be remembered correctly, or the way you wished it had happened. Either way, your story does make Bluffton a good place to miss.

—*Rudi and Fred Steiner*

Meet the writers

Tobias Buckell is a New York Times Bestselling and World Fantasy Award-winning author born in the Caribbean. His novels and over 70 stories are translated into 19 different languages. His work has been nominated for the Hugo Award, Nebula Award, World Fantasy Award and the Astounding Award for Best New Science Fiction Author. He lives in Bluffton with his wife and twin daughters.

Rick Emmert grew up by a farm pond beside Riley Creek two miles south of Bluffton. He graduated from Bluffton High School in 1968, and later from Earlham College and Tokyo University of Arts, where he studied Japanese and Asian performance. Based in Tokyo, he has performed and taught Japanese classical noh theatre all over the world, founded a professional theatre company to perform noh in English, and has written a series of books on noh for Tokyo's National Noh Theatre. Recently retired after teaching 34 years at Musashino University, he has returned regularly to visit family and friends in the Bluffton area.

Dave Essinger teaches creative writing and edits the literary magazine Slippery Elm at the University of Findlay, and lives in Bluffton with his wife Alice and two children, June and Levin. His first novel, Running Out, came out from Main Street Rag Publishing Company in 2017, and he's been working on his next book since then. Find him online at www.dave-essinger.com. "Winter Liminal" was first published by Great Lakes Review's Narrative Map Project, at http://greatlakesreview.org/category/nonfiction-words/narrative-map-project/.

Ron Geiser is a native of Bluffton who has been a high school athlete, youth coach, sports historian and statistician for both the high school and university. He was only the second non-coach or athlete selected to Bluffton University's Athletic Hall of Fame. He was editor of the Bluffton News from 1974 to 1978 and was communications director at BC for 15 years and assisted with sports information another 10. Now a widower, he was married to BHS grads Arlene Balmer (52 years) and then Loretta Nonnamaker Creeger (2 1/2 years).

Jeff Gundy and his family have lived in Bluffton since he came to teach English at Bluffton College in 1984. He studied at Goshen College and Indiana University, but four of his siblings and at least a dozen uncles, aunts, and assorted cousins graduated from Bluffton, plus several nieces and nephews. He has published eight books of poems and four prose books, and was named Ohio Poet of the Year for Somewhere Near Defiance (Anhinga, 2014). He spent his last two sabbaticals at the University of Salzburg on a Fulbright Lectureship and at LCC International University in Klaipeda, Lithuania, but has settled back into his place on South Lawn Avenue.

Charles Hilty (1934-2020), a Bluffton High School 1952 graduate, was editor of the Bluffton News from 1961 to 1967. During his editorship he was president of the Bluffton-Richland Public Library board. He was night editor of the St. Louis Post-Dispatch from 1973-1978, and a senior staff member for U.S. Congressman Ed Madigan of Illinois from 1978-1991. After President George H.W. Bush appointed Madigan as Secretary of Agriculture in 1991, Hilty was appointed Assistant Secretary of Agriculture for Administration and served as such for the balance of Bush's term.

Robert Kreider (1919-2015) grew up in Bluffton during his formative years of 1929 to 1935 when his father was pastor of First Mennonite Church. He earned a master's degree in social ethics and later a doctorate in European history both from the University of Chicago. He joined the Bluffton College faculty in 1954, became academic dean in 1965, and president from 1965 to 1972. He was on the faculty of Bethel College, North Newton, Kansas, as professor of peace studies and director of the Mennonite Library and Archives from 1975 until his retirement in 1985.

Brendon Matthews, a community banker in Bluffton, grew up in the big white farmhouse on the Bluffton University Nature Preserve, was an All-Ohio soccer player for Bluffton High School, and graduated from BHS in 1998. After a stint in Anderson, Indiana, where he earned an English degree and an MBA from Anderson University, he moved back to Bluffton with his wife, Renee, in 2006. He has coached youth soccer teams including teams for all three of his daughters, and he is a volunteer assistant coach for the BHS girls' soccer team. He is also a doctoral candidate in an Interdisciplinary Leadership program at Creighton University.

Ruth Bundy Naylor arrived in Bluffton as a coed in 1952 then left in 1954 when her fiancé, Stan Naylor, graduated. They returned in 1968 with their two young children, Kim and Jeff. Ruth then graduated from BC with a degree in Comprehensive English and taught at Bluffton High School for 12 years. At the invitation of Bluffton's First Mennonite Church, Ruth served on the pastoral staff for 12 years. She has published two books of poetry, A Family Affair and Straw & All: A Christmas Poetry Collection, as well as FAITH TALK: a spiritual memoir inviting reflection and dialogue.

Joanne Niswander says Bluffton has been "home" to her more than any other place in her 90-plus years. From life on a farm in central Illinois, she came to Bluffton College and met and married a Bluffton native. After living elsewhere for 26 years, the Niswanders returned to Bluffton in 1990. While music (organ and voice) filled her early life, she later turned to writing, which still keeps her at her computer. From 1990 to 2010 she wrote monthly columns for the Bluffton News, and then occasionally for the Bluffton Icon. Two published books kept her writing after that.

Rick Ramseyer grew up in Bluffton, is a 1979 Bluffton High School graduate, and a graduate of Bluffton University and the University of Missouri School of Journalism. A former staff writer for the Bluffton News, he has extensive experience as a daily newspaper reporter, magazine editor and communications specialist. Rick is writing a book about a landmark citizenship case and has worked on it during two residencies at the Hewnoaks Artist Colony in western Maine. He and his wife, Beth, live in Maine and have two daughters.

Carolyn Urich Rich grew up in a small Indiana town. It was a family tradition to attend Bluffton College, where her father was on the Board of Trustees. She fell in love with the Bluffton community and assured her permanence here by marrying a local boy, Joe Urich. She's known for her art projects and church and community volunteer activities. She was taught by three generations of Luginbuhls...Darvin, Gregg and most recently a class by Kat. In addition to raising two children, she enjoyed over 20 years working in the Student Life and Registrar's Offices at Bluffton University. Following Joe's death, she married John Rich, whose teaching at BC years ago made moving to Bluffton very enticing.

David Rempel Smucker was born in Bluffton to Carl and Irene (Yoder) Smucker. He graduated from Bluffton High School in 1967. After graduate school, he worked as a historian (editor, researcher, speaker) at Lancaster Mennonite Historical Society in Lancaster, Pennsylvania, for more than 20 years, then moved to Manitoba, Canada, where his wife, Judith, was born and raised. They have two married children and two grandchildren who live in Wisconsin and New York.

Jill Steinmetz was born in Bluffton to Teri (Miller) and Joel Steinmetz. At Bluffton High School, she led her soccer team to a NWC championship and designed the Class of '14 commencement program. After graduating with a degree in Graphic Design and Spanish from Goshen College, she served with Mennonite Central Committee as a digital media specialist in Honduras. She currently lives in Columbus, Ohio, where she works as a freelance graphic designer.

Acknowledgments

Countless people played a part in this book's compilation.

Mary Pannabecker Steiner, my wife, whose seemingly most frequent 2020 comment to me follows: "Are you still working on that book?" deserves accolades I can never repay.

The late **Charles Hilty's** and **Richard Jordan's** observations of the Bluffton scene over the decades spoke volumes and their voices are missed.

The late **Robert Kreider's** writings continue to inspire and remind us of the values of our community's past.

Contributing writers, whose essays are now part of the growing Bluffton oral tradition, deserve an encore. Thank you, each one of you.

Jill Steinmetz, graphic designer, created the cover and formatted the material inside the cover in a most professional way. The world will see more of her creative projects in years to come.

Elizabeth Gordon-Hancock served as the final proof-reader. Few people with such a grasp of grammar as she has could handle this role with the spirit she approaches her work.

The variations of What me – worry?
Alfred E. Neuman, the iconic mascot and cover boy of Mad magazine, is always pictured with his motto.

"What, me worry?" "What – me worry?" "What, Me Worry?" "What – Me Worry?" And "Me Worry?" have been used interchangeably since the 1950s. All are correct, making the popular culture catchphrase even more idiotic. We chose the version "What me – worry?" as our usage in this book. We decided to ignore the Mad magazine statement: "It's crackers to slip a rozzer the dropsy in snide." That would have required an additional chapter.

As an additional aside, we also chose not to include an essay about a man who called himself LoBagola, who lectured at Bluffton College in the 1930s. We own an autographed copy of his autobiography and recall once in an email that Robert Kreider rediscovered his name used as an adjective in an article in The New Yorker. Perhaps in the next book.

Rudi Steiner   *Fred Steiner*

Rudi Steiner stands with Bluffton's oldest business storefront sign. It originally hung on the window of the store of his great-grandfather, Rudolf Althaus, circa 1890. Fred Steiner stands in front of the earliest known Main Street Bluffton photograph, taken by Will Triplett also circa 1890.

Other books by Fred Steiner

Town at the Fork of The Rileys Revisited
  An update of the 1961 *Town at the Fork of The Rileys*
Published in 1986
By the Bluffton News, out of print

A Century of Pirates
Commemorating the 125th anniversary of the Bluffton News
Published in 2000
By The Bluffton News, out-of-print

Bluffton, A Good Place to Miss – Bluffton stories 1900-1975
Published in 2012
By WorkPlay Publishing
ISBN 978-0-9842122-4-8

The Bluffton We Never Knew:
  Photographs from our first half century, 1861-1911
Published in 2017
By WorkPlay Publishing
ISBN: 0990554570

190

CPSIA information can be obtained
at www.ICGtesting.com
Printed in the USA
FSHW010837291120